Directing a play

Yoma Sasburgh in *Hippolytus*

DIRECTING A PLAY

James Roose-Evans on the art of directing and acting

FOREWORD BY VANESSA REDGRAVE

Theatre Arts Books New York

For my mother and father in gratitude

The quotations from *Under Milk Wood* by Dylan Thomas are reprinted with the permission of J. M. Dent & Sons Ltd, London, and the Trustees for the Copyrights of the late Dylan Thomas, and New Directions, New York, Copyright 1954 by New Directions Publishing Corporation.

The extracts from *The Seagull* by Anton Chekhov are from *The Seagull Produced by Stanislavski* translated by David Magarshack and are reprinted with permission of David Magarshack, Dennis Dobson Publishers, London, and Theatre Arts Books, New York. All rights reserved.

The extracts from *Témoignage sur le Théâtre* by Louis Jouvet (originally published in *Theatre Arts Monthly*) are reprinted with permission of Librairie Ernest Flammarion, Paris, and Theatre Arts Books, New York.

The extract from *The Flower in Drama and Glamour* by Stark Young is reprinted with permission of Charles Scribner's Sons, New York.

The extract from *My Life in Art* by Constantin Stanislavski is reprinted with permission of Theatre Arts Books, New York, and Geoffrey Bles Ltd, London.

Thanks are due to the following for their permission to reproduce pictures:
Helen Craig for pls 20, 27; John Haynes for pls 7–15, 17–19, 28; John Vere Brown for pls 21–26, 55–59; and the title-page illustration; Les Editions Nomis for pl 35; Duell, Sloan and Pearce Inc. New York, for pl 29; Barbara Wilkes for pl 4; Michael Cox for pls 1–3, 16, 42–49.

The sets for *Cider with Rosie* (The Garrick Theatre), *Murder in the Cathedral* (Belgrade Theatre, Coventry), *The Marriage of Saint Francis* (The Maddermarket Theatre, Norwich), *Paradise Lost* (Vanbrugh Theatre), *Hippolytus* and *Letters from an Eastern Front* (Hampstead Theatre Club) were designed by the author.

Other sets were as follows: *The Admirable Crichton* and *The Taming of the Shrew*—Joan Jefferson Farjeon; *Nathan and Tabileth*—Harry Waistnage; *The Two Character Play*—Peter Rice; *Adventures in the Skin Trade*—Michael Young; *The Seagull*—John Gunter; *Circus Boy*—Christopher Morley; *The Little Clay Cart*—Barbara Wilkes.

The costumes for *Hippolytus* were designed by Dawn Pavitt; for *The Little Clay Cart* and *The Taming of the Shrew* by Jack Notman; for *Cider with Rosie* by David Walker.

First published in 1968 by Theatre Arts Books, 333 Sixth Avenue,
New York, NY 10014
Published in Great Britain by Studio Vista Ltd
Blue Star House, Highgate Hill, London N19
Set in 'Monotype' Bembo 12 pt.
Printed in Great Britain by
Richard Clay (The Chaucer Press), Ltd,
Bungay, Suffolk

Contents

Enter Quince, Snug, Bottom, Flute, Snout and Starveling.

QUINCE: Is all our company here?

A Midsummer Night's Dream

Foreword

Dear Jimmie,

Why do I have to call this a foreword? I wouldn't have written any of this if I hadn't read your book. Your book is so *useful*, I like that very much. It's a good detailed guide map of the territories of the director; the freeways, arterials, roads and lanes; and your personal discoveries are places 'well worth a visit'. I do wish I could have seen your production of *Under Milk Wood*, by the way; I wish I could have acted in it.

But really I want to write to you about the duties of the actor to his director and playwright; because when I had read Chapter 3 'The Director and the Actor' I was stimulated to put into some kind of order many stray thoughts and experiences on the subject of this relationship. I felt very ashamed when I read your words 'he (the director) must be prepared to accept defeat with humour and humility. A director has to work with other human beings whose sense of dedication, in the main, is not even comparable with that of a dancer or a singer. The average actor relies on a minimum of technique....'

As you say, an actor may be compared to a dancer in so much as his body must be free and responsive to the inner impulses; and I agree, as a rule we actors do not have the *dedication to* disciplined and continual technical practice, without which the dancer or musician simply cannot function. I trained for six years as a classical dancer. I remember, my muscles remember, the remorseless repetition of exercises; only this kind of work could prepare for a few moments when the trained muscles could respond to the imagination, and something approaching interpretation could be reached for.

You refer to Tyrone Guthrie demanding two octaves vocal range of the actor. I watched him direct Zoë Caldwell as Helena in *All's Well That Ends Well*; he gave her precise instruction on changes of pitch and rhythm which she worked hard to achieve, and as the days went by she absorbed these technical impositions until there was no effort but delightful and exciting spontaneity. Guthrie has an expert musical ear so he can give directions which very few other directors are capable of either conceiving or relaying; and Zoë must be one of the very few actresses who are willing to accept such direction, or who are technically *able* to take such direction.

You say that 'the art of directing is also an art of compromise, of diplomacy', and later on 'the director has to strive ceaselessly for perfection and, simultaneously, know when and how to compromise'. No, no, no! As an actor, I say 'no, don't compromise because of us'. I say to myself 'make sure not to be the cause of compromise between

6

the director and his vision of the play'. How many times have I argued (a more accurate word than 'discussed') an interpretation of a scene. I have quite sincerely believed I was serving the playwright. I was *wrong*. The director must be the sole interpreter of the writer; if he is forced to compromise by an actor's conscious or subconscious refusal to execute a direction, then the play as it ultimately appears to an audience will be blurred. I am supposing naturally that the director has 'done his homework' as we say. Possibly it may be true that the director should diplomatically compromise for the sake of helping an actor's confidence; but I think that a more solid confidence is achieved when the actor accepts the discipline of a sterner demand upon his technique and imagination.

The 'great' actors are all 'obedient' actors; their temperament is put to the service of the play and the director. Quietly industrious, they seem to put their whole effort into doing what the director asks, *then* understanding it. I don't agree any more that there *must* be a motivation for everything an actor is asked to say or do, nor that he must know it before speaking or moving. Examination of motives preceding action came about in reaction to perfunctory and clichéd work. It is helpful as an antidote for a fatigued or lazy imagination. In fact, as we know, a great deal of human behaviour is the outward expression of inherited or conditioned reflexes. The fascination and the power of human intelligence is that we question these reflexes and try to change them. I am in deep water and quite unequipped to write about this, but I'll try and be more precise. None of us can be quite sure how we will react in a given situation, or under unusual conditions. Knowledge of how we *have* behaved is a guide but no more. We are more surprising than perhaps we give ourselves credit for; which is why, in the theatre, I think the play, the scene, the character, will be more enriched by actions or moves given by the director which do not *at that moment* seem to be logical, or correctly motivated. Jean-Luc Godard says something about turning the truth upside down and liking it better, and *deliberately* doing it. I like that too.

Jimmie, I must stop. Probably I should have stopped sooner. This seems more like a letter, which it is really because I daren't call this anything as grand as a 'foreword'. I worked with you when I was a student, and your book makes me want to work with you again.

Vanessa Redgrave

7

The director, when he is also the producer, first selects the play, distributes the parts to the actors of his choice, designs (or has designed for him) the rough models of the settings and costumes, oversees their making and during all this time organizes and manages rehearsals. He determines the entrances and exits, the positions of the actors, serving as choreographer to that dance which is the sum of the play's movements; he regulates the off-stage noises, the music, the lighting. In short, he arranges in ensemble and in detail all the generalities and and all the particulars of that complex ceremony which the performance will be.

LOUIS JOUVET

1 Planning a production

The planning and preparation of a production is comparable to that of a garden. The gardener studies the layout of the land and tries to discover the design that is innate to the landscape. He may impose a design, creating something highly artificial which may be totally successful as a garden although alien to that landscape. So, too, in the theatre.

The director's main task is to understand his author, to seek, not to impose a style, but to unearth the form within—like a sculptor faced with a block of marble. The first impression of a play, therefore, can be very important, and often, as one reads, it is helpful to jot down odd impressions, colours, shapes, patterns of movement, sound, a key phrase to be underlined—yet one should read swiftly, lightly, like a kestrel hovering over a valley. Later readings will analyze and take the play to pieces, but on that first acquaintance one is exploring, as it were, the face of a new love. Later, one will discover in that face other faces, other aspects and then, finally, the many will merge once again into the one face of the known person, as in a Picasso painting one sees both the whole face and its many aspects and angles.

The director seeks the heart of a play, the reason for its having been created. The search is always for the original design. What was the author trying to say? Why was it necessary for him to write this play? Why was it written at this moment of time? What relevance has it to life today? On the surface one examines the narrative, the story line, and then, delving deeper, the sub plot, the motivation of the characters, the inner action of the play and, finally, its significance within a sociological and spiritual context. Continued readings and prolonged thought are required, since first impressions are not infallible. When I first read Sir James Barrie's *The Admirable Crichton* I was beguiled into thinking this a slight, charming period comedy, its message no longer applicable in a changed social milieu. Subsequent readings, however, revealed that this was a far more subtle, considerably more serious play; not only brilliantly constructed —Barrie is always a fine craftsman—but a fantasy etched in acid and disturbing in its final impact.

I began by jettisoning all attempts at the kind of naturalistic staging envisaged by Barrie, who was writing at a time when the new ideas of Craig had not permeated the London theatre. In the original production real grass, bamboo and water were used in the second act. Instead, I asked my designer, Joan Jefferson Farjeon, to give me for the first act a circular mauve carpet, surrounded by a white Edwardian circus cage (pl 1). Light shone into this space from all sides, but beyond was darkness. The central doors opened and closed automatically, and within the cage the aristocratic animals moved beautifully, with an apparent sense of freedom, yet trapped by their circle of social conventions. Barrie has sub-titled this act 'The Other Island'.

In the second act, rather than convert the entire stage into the desert island, I had the designer limit the island to the central portion of the stage, leaving the rest to represent the sea (pl 2). I wanted to emphasize the initial sense of strain for these ship-wrecked aristocrats. Stripped of their finery, they have to learn to live at close quarters; they are forced to adapt to new circumstances, to evolve new attitudes, fresh conventions, so that by the third act, which Barrie calls 'The Happy Home', when the set covers the entire stage, it is as though the island has grown with their growth as individuals (pl 3). It is, however, a fragile growth, and with the fourth act we see how easily they settle back into their old cage. In order to stress this turning back of the clock the actors wore the same costumes as in Act 1, while (following Barrie's instructions) relics of their island life adorned the walls of the cage, fossilized into sentimental memories. Only the continuing presence of Crichton disturbs them so that they all feel that they are 'sitting on the edge of a volcano'. Crichton, the artist in life, has disturbed their usual routine, and it is only with his departure that they can utter a sigh of relief and settle back comfortably into their usual rut.

Without sentimentality, Barrie shows that whatever may be learned on the islands of our visions must be tested in the arenas of daily life. Ideals must be made realities or they are worth nothing. With his extraordinary irony Barrie reveals how little we learn, how unreliable is enthusiasm, how temporary emotion. Gently, ironically, the play sounds the break-up of the social values of the Victorian and Edwardian eras and the inevitable emergence of new ideas and a new class—Crichton, although born into service ('the son of a butler and a lady's maid—perhaps the happiest of all combinations'), leaves in order to marry Tweeny and becomes the successful owner of a public house. It is a period play that transcends its period.

When I was at the Maddermarket Theatre in Norwich I designed and directed Henri Gheon's *The Marriage of Saint Francis*. The first and obvious thought was to stage this after the paintings of Giotto, since the play is a series of meditations on the life and passion of St Francis of Assisi and his marriage to Lady Poverty. However, St Francis has been fossilized by the faithful into a popular sentimental image. The beautiful medieval village church of Storgursey in the Quantocks was for years buried under Victorian pseudo-Gothic; once the accretion of years of piety or misuse is scraped away there is discovered underneath the true identity of a building or of a person. So with St Francis. He was a romantic, an intense individualist, but also he was a rebel, a non-conformist, a constant embarrassment, who taught that one must live from day to day, literally taking no thought for the morrow but improvising with what comes to hand. It was these qualities that I wanted to emphasize. I wanted the audience to become involved with Francis and not merely to come out of the theatre saying, 'Wasn't it beautiful!'

The floor of the stage was painted a rich reddish earth brown, while against a white cyclorama there was a simple structure made of unplaned, unpainted lengths of timber, like the first posts of a wooden house, such as one may see being constructed in the Tyrol. Within this framework mobile units made of bamboo, in the shape of arches and doorways, were moved about by the actors. Four square blocks provided seats or became the blocks of stone for the rebuilding of St Damian's, or a well in the piazza. A wooden bench served also as a footbridge over a deep ravine. In the second act all that was required to suggest the chapel of St Damian were three arches, each smaller than the other, placed one in front of the other, and at the end a small bamboo cross before which Francis knelt (pl 4). No properties were used, so the audience were compelled to participate imaginatively in what was happening. They experienced a sense of imaginative release, the freedom of improvisation, of having at one and the same time everything and nothing. Such is the essence of St Francis's credo.

When I first saw *Under Milk Wood* at the New Theatre in London I found myself distracted by the visual detail of the set: the many small trucks that were shunted on and off. Nothing had been left to the imagination. If an actor said—'Miles away a dog barks', then sure enough, one heard a dog barking. When the Narrator described Mary Ann Sailors 'ducking under the gippo's clothes pegs', there was the washing on the line and the old lady bending beneath it. By the time Lord Cut-Glass's roomful of ticking clocks had been trucked on to the stage we had missed half of the Narrator's description. It was as though the directors had been afraid to trust the text, rich in imagery and comedy as it is, and felt that they must elaborate and proliferate lest the audience become bored. About halfway through the performance I closed my eyes and listened to the rest of the play. It was this experience that set me pondering the problem of staging a play written expressly for another medium. *Under Milk Wood* was commissioned by the BBC, and first presented at the YMHA auditorium in New York as a concert reading, with the actors on high stools and their scripts on lecterns. Dylan Thomas has provided his own clue to the work in its sub-title—'A Play for Voices'. So it was that when I came to stage the play, first at the RADA's Vanbrugh Theatre and subsequently at the Lyric Theatre, Hammersmith, there was no scenery and the actors were grouped in a tight phalanx on a rising plane of chairs with a narrator on either side. Each actor played many parts; there was no make-up or character costuming.

No one left the stage. The actors rose or stood on chairs, leaned forward, mimed, rang their own bells, blew their own soap bubbles, provided their own cock-crows, played their own mouth organs, made their own sound effects. All was contained within the company so that the hill of chairs became the village of Llaregyb; and because each actor played many parts, with the exceptions of Captain Cat and Polly Garter, one had the feeling of generations of families, all the shared memories of a community, and that total lack of privacy that one finds in any village. All participated in the dramas and comedies of the rest; the songs that they sang were the songs that had been handed down from one generation to another. When the entire cast, rocking from side to side, sang 'Johnny Crack and Flossie Snail' they were both the children of the village at that particular moment and, at the same time, their parents and the older folk recalling these songs of their childhood.

The entire play is a canticle of praise by a religious poet, and its theme is contained in the words of the Rev. Eli Jenkins's evening prayer:

> We are not wholly bad or good
> Who live our lives under Milk Wood,
> And Thou I know wilt be the first
> To see our best side not our worst.

Without passing moral judgment, Dylan Thomas observes humanity with humour and compassion:

> And all your deeds and words,
> Each truth, each lie,
> Die in unjudging love.

In rehearsal a great deal of improvisation was used in order to open up the individual characterizations. The entire cast was always present at these sessions, sharing, as it were, in the community's collective memories (many of the improvisations showed the various characters at different stages of their lives). Once this had been achieved, however, the company sat in their rows of chairs and were literally conducted, passage by passage, line by line, sound by sound, going back and over the phrasing of a particular line, the length of a pause, or the pitch of different voices, the exact balance of a sound, a word or an inflection. The lighting or extinguishing of a cigarette, the picking up or putting down of knitting, was all carefully blocked so that nothing would distract in this mosaic of sound. All was 'plotted and pieced'; yet within this austere form the greatest freedom was achieved. In this production the director closely resembled a conductor, and always I had in mind some of the finest and most disciplined Welsh choirs.

Often, when I was contemplating that hill of empty chairs in *Under Milk Wood* which, at the curtain call, always seemed so vibrantly alive with the presence of the absent actors, I would ponder what would happen if the chairs could move, could become more intimately a part of the action. Thus it was that in Laurie Lee's *Cider with Rosie* the chairs became members of the cast and, like the actors, played many parts. Their use in this production was a logical and imaginative extension of their use in the production of *Under Milk Wood*.

For *Cider with Rosie*, which was presented at the Garrick Theatre in 1963, I designed an oval-shaped rostrum tilted towards the audience, like an enormous mill-stone, and painted a golden sand colour. One foot off the ground at the front, it rose to a height of four feet at the back so that the actors had to manipulate a steep rake, suggestive of the hills of Stroud and that steep bank upon which the Lee cottage stood; while the circular shape suggested the valley, and that womb of village and family life out of which the poet emerged. Suspended above this golden disc was an object like a large edelweiss flower, made of ears of wheat and strips of wood, an object suggestive of the sun and moon and stars of childhood, poised, luminous, above the valley. The action of this 'bucolic ritual', as Harold Hobson so aptly described it in *The Sunday Times* (it was never meant to be a play), unfolded on the disc, against a cyclorama, employing black tabs for the night scenes. It was a production that depended upon the vitality and flexibility of the actors, an imaginative use of a few properties and a subtle use of lighting which, at certain moments, achieved an effect of extraordinary luminosity. One such moment occurred during the scene of Granny Wallon's wine-making, when the disc, revolving with patterns of white petals, became a vast vat, while across the cyclorama rich colours slid and merged like a Chagall painting on the move, evoking the poet's description of 'what seasons fermented in Granny Wallon's kitchen. What summers were brought to the boil . . . the vats boiled daily in their suds of sugar, revolving petals in throbbing water, seething in purple vats, while the air aromatic, steamy, embalmed, distilled the hot dews and flowery soups and ran the wines down the dripping walls.'

For the scene depicting the young Laurie Lee in bed with his mother, the arrangement of six chairs—three at the head, three at the foot—with a green cloth spread like a counterpane over the two actors, suggested the double bed. Similarly, the chairs quickly became the rows of desks at the village school or, when placed in pairs down the slope of the rostrum with the entire cast waving handkerchiefs and singing 'One man went to mow a meadow', the charabanc taking the village on its annual outing to Weston-super-Mare. When the chairs were placed on the perimeter of the disc, the actors sitting astride, alternately rising and falling to the accompaniment of hurdy-gurdy music and flashing, revolving coloured lights, the whole stage became the roundabout at the fair. Placed end to end and with low lighting through the bars of the chair-backs casting tiger stripes of shadows across the disc, they became a winter hedge at sunset; and when the chairs were set upside down, slanting diagonally across the rostrum, they became the sheaves of corn in the field where Laurie drinks cider with Rosie (pls 7—15).

Louis Jouvet once wrote:

'In the limbo where the production takes form, in the slow growth during which its features are shaped, where it is foreseen in imagination, where the dramatic leaven is mysteriously at work, the director watches with patience, discretion and tenderness over the straggling elements he has assembled to give life to the playwright's work. His job is accomplished through intuition, understanding, foresight, through a special alchemy composed of words, sounds, gestures, colours, lines, movements, rhythms and silences, and including an imponderable which will radiate the proper feeling of laughter or emotion when the work appears before the public.'

Although in a good production the overall concept of the play, the basic style and much of the detail will stem from the director, in the final design it should prove impossible to separate the various threads contributed by the director, the designer, the author, the actors and the technical staff. A good production is like a seamless robe. The production of a play is a collaborative exercise resembling most the heaping up of all the children's hands, all the family's hands, on the parental knee in the game one used to play by the fireside when young.

2 Blocking a production

Where the director is not his own designer it is his task to talk with the designer about the play, explaining his concept and vision of the whole, as well as the intended style of the production. The designer will make sketches, or build a model of the set, which he and the director will then discuss. Often it is a matter of trial and error. One idea will lead to another. The original concept may be scrapped altogether and an entirely different approach found. The director may have no more than a vague idea as to what the set should look like, in which case he will rely upon the designer to create a satisfactory environment for the actors. Gradually, the final design of the set and the costumes emerges, and once it is agreed upon, the designer will make a detailed model, working drawings and a ground plan, for the carpenter; while he will begin shopping for materials with the wardrobe mistress.

The director will tell the designer what furniture and property are needed, while the designer will indicate the additional furniture and props used to dress the set, in case the director wishes to incorporate them into the production. The director will need to check the size of everything. The size of a kitchen table will determine how much space is available around it, in relation to the set and the other furniture used, as as well how many props may be used on it. The designer may announce that he has discovered 'a lovely piece of furniture', only to be told that it is no good for the action required. Delicate period chairs are no good if the actors have to stand on them, throw them about, or if they have to be sat on by heavy actors and so on. It is no good the director leaving this until the dress rehearsal. As likely as not it will then be too late to change anything. The basic positioning of the furniture is also something the director has to settle before he can begin to block in the moves for the actors. In a naturalistic set he will have to imagine where and how the furniture would be placed by the characters in that environment, at that time of day, year or period. If there is only one set, the re-arrangement of furniture in one act, providing it is logical, will create a great variety of blocking.

'In every good director,' Meyerhold once said, 'there potentially sits a dramatist.' It is not merely that the director often has to edit a play, suggesting cuts, alterations, re-writes, but in imagining the action of the play, seeing it in his mind's eye already taking place on the stage, he has to possess the story-teller's art. It is he who sets the play in motion, creating a choreography for the actors, planning their entrances and exits, their moves and business.

If it is a stylized production he will draw upon modern dance techniques, mime, music-hall routines, *Commedia dell'Arte*, ballet, the Chinese classical theatre, the Kathakali dance dramas, ethnic dances and ceremonials from all parts of the world, puppets and marionettes, shadow puppets, film and projection. Similarly, as accompaniment, he will draw from classical and modern music, jazz and percussion, *musique-concrète*, songs, choruses, chants, cries, groans, sounds.

In a naturalistic production he will need to relate to reality as he has observed it. Because the theatre is not reality itself, but the illusion of, he will select and compose aspects of reality. In real life a woman might be seated at the sink peeling potatoes and talking to another person in the room, with her back to that person. But you could not play a whole scene like that in the theatre. Not only would it mean the actress having to use much more vocal projection—a basic rule when an actor turns upstage—but the other actor would have to play upstage for most of the scene. This means that all the audience would see would be the backs and sides of the two actors' heads.

There used to be a rule that you should never act with your back to the audience. The school of naturalism has rightly rejected that and insisted upon the presence of the fourth wall. Instead of the actor consciously playing out front to the audience, he imagines a fourth wall to the set, so that when he faces front he is looking not at the audience but at doors, furniture, pictures or through windows on to imagined views and landscapes. The audience is listening and looking in as through a key-hole. In a naturalistic production, therefore, the actor will often turn his back to the audience, yet there is a limit as to how long this can be done without losing the audience's attention. In acting, as in real life, the eyes reveal a great deal. We need to see the actor's face and so, in our imagined scene of two people in a kitchen, the director would have to adapt the reality of life to the reality of art. Either the sink would have to be moved down-stage, so that the actress could sit sideways on to it and look across her shoulder at the other person or else the director would have to suggest to the actress that she bring her basin of potatoes down to the kitchen table. Alternatively, he could commence the scene with the actress upstage, her back to the audience, perhaps filling the basin with water, and then have her move downstage to the table to start peeling. Later in the scene, perhaps in order to emphasize a point in the dialogue, or *a moment* between the two characters, he could have the actress rise, wipe her hands on her apron and move across to the stove, either to check the meat roasting in the oven or to put the potatoes on to boil.

The director must 'break the action', because, in general, if an actor stays in the same position for too long without moving the audience is likely to become bored and rest-less. Just as a new thought requires a change of tone in the voice, a new inflection, so, too, in any one scene there will be subtle shifts of body positions, and groupings, all serving to focus attention upon the significant action. It is here that, when blocking a play, a director may find the use of *an interrupted action* useful, in order to bring an added emphasis to a particular line or moment. A character may rise, move towards the door, then pause and turn back as he remembers something else he wants to say. A character may start to pour tea, then pause to make a remark before carrying on with the action. In each case the interrupted action draws attention to what is being said, or to what is happening on stage, and the subsequent completion of the action serves to underline this. It is rather like a post-script in a letter.

While blocking his production beforehand the director is generally able to foresee any masking problems, and to adjust the movements accordingly. If furniture or actors mask part of the action from the audience for only a brief while this does not matter, since when the piece of furniture is moved aside, or the actors shift their positions, the actor who is momentarily masked will then come into fresh focus. What is important is that, at no point, should a key scene, or the actor dominating the stage at that moment, be masked from the audience. Repeatedly, at rehearsals, the director will need to move about the theatre, checking from the sides of the auditorium, and from upstairs in the circle and the gallery, that every member of the audience can see. If there is any serious masking he will then have to call out to the actor—'Over to stage left a bit! Upstage a fraction! Open up there, out a bit!'—stage left and right always being the actor's left and right.

Given a scene between two actors it would be very monotonous for the audience if they had to sit and look at the profiles of the actors for any length of time. Although centre-stage is the strongest position in which an actor can stand, even this will pall if he stays there too long. If two actors are facing each other in profile the one who is speaking will find places in the text where he can swing his head round to face out front, or turn away from the other actor, shifting the angle of his body so that he opens out the scene for the audience. In real life we do not always gaze steadfastly into the face of the person to whom we are talking. Often we may be tying up a shoelace, lighting a cigarette, looking out of the window, watching someone go by or merely turned away deep in thought. When two actors are playing in profile the director will need to check, moreover, that neither is masking the other. It may be that they are standing too close to each other, or that one is standing a fraction too downstage of the other and so masking him for the audience on his side. Sometimes it is merely a matter of the actor's stance and where he has placed his feet. The placing of the feet determines the angle of the body, and if the actor opens his feet he will at once open up his position. Young actors in particular often hate being told about this kind of thing. They like to be carried away on a flood of emotion, and regard it as artificial to have to think about where they stand, how they stand and so on. But the whole of acting is artifice, and technique is made up of a thousand such details.

What an actor does in a scene is really a matter of actor and director *imagining* what the character would do in that particular situation. Unless he is directing a musical or an opera, the experienced director is unlikely to block the whole play in advance. Given his own experience, his study of the play and experienced actors with whom to work, the movement of the play should unfold of its own accord, growing out of the imagined reality of each scene. But the young or inexperienced director needs to block in advance, working either with a model of the set and cut-out figures or using a ground-plan, pencilling in the positions of the furniture, and using chessmen for the actors. In any one scene there is always a variety of possible moves, as in a chess game, and the more he has thought these out in advance, the quicker he will be able to respond to that recurring question, 'Where shall I move?'—the more so if his actors are inexperienced. The director ought always to be able to suggest more than one alternative to an actor. Like trying on a coat, the actor may need to try one move after another before he finds one that fits. Blocking a play in advance, a valuable exercise in itself for the young director, is an arduous task. Because, in the early days of the Moscow Art Theatre, he had to work with inexperienced actors, Stanislavski used to work out a whole production in advance, like a musical score. His prompt copies for *The Seagull* and *Othello*, translated by David Magarshack and Dr Helen Novak respectively, ought to be studied by every young director.

There are available editions of plays which are based upon the prompt copies of West End productions. These are used a good deal by amateur groups, but they only provide the moves, and not the motivation for the moves. Besides, what works for one actor does not necessarily work for another. This is why, when a director revives a production, he should be prepared to abandon the original moves and to explore the play afresh with a new set of actors.

Having achieved a naturalistic blocking of a play, the director must have an eye to the composition of the stage pictures. Few critics are sensitive to the visual or choreographic aspects of a production. The action should flow from one picture to another, as was superbly demonstrated in the Berliner Ensemble's production of *Coriolanus*. Many of the groupings will happen spontaneously, but others will need to be selected and composed by the director.

Like a choreographer, the director may even have to place individual actors. There are always some actors who are very inhibited in terms of movement, whose bodies are like Dutch dolls, very wooden, with stiff arms. Because of muscular or nervous tension, they do not act with their bodies, but propel themselves from position to position while speaking the lines. If the director cannot release the actor by means of imaginative stimuli he may have to show him what is required, or even give him specific things to do with his arms and hands to relate him physically to the furniture or the props. Given a table, the actor can lean on it, sit on it, perch on it, rest on it, sit at it. The character may be tidying his hair, fingering his tie, scratching his ear, picking his nose, taking up a newspaper, twiddling a pencil, have both hands behind his neck or in his trouser pockets, or be standing with one hand touching another piece of furniture. Whatever the director gives the actor to do must, of course, be related to the character he is playing and that particular scene. The more the actor can relate to physical objects, the more he is enabled to relax, to concentrate upon and believe in the reality of the imagined environment on stage.

If, at such moments, the director can be likened to a choreographer, the actor may certainly be compared with a dancer. Guthrie requires of an actor that he be able to cover two octaves vocally; few can. Similarly, few actors have control over their body, are able to use it like an instrument, responding to whatever demands are made upon it by the creative imagination. Few realize the importance of gesture.

3 The director and the actor

At the first rehearsal the designer should be present to explain to the actors and stage management the model of the set, and to show them the costume designs. This helps everyone to visualize what the production will look like. If the play is a period revival books and pictures about the period should be lying around, and during rehearsals the director may choose to read extracts from such books in order to stimulate the actors towards a greater identification with the background of the play. If the actors do not know each other there should be time for them to chat, drink coffee and have a cigarette. From the start there should be the feeling that this is a team.

The basic style of a production will emerge during rehearsals as a result of the director's notes, but it may be helpful to the actor to know beforehand what he is aiming at, whether a naturalistic or stylized production and, if the latter, what particular style. Sometimes the director may commence with a straight read-through of the play with everyone seated around a large table or in a circle. However, it is important that such a reading should not attempt to be a performance. Actors are often tempted to act it up on such occasions, and much damage can be done by forcing an emotion. At the same time, however, it is from a first reading in company with his fellow actors that an actor often gains valuable intuitive insights into the play; he sees his part more clearly in relation to the other characters and to the play as a whole. For the director such a reading can be useful in that it reveals to him the needs and problems and positive contributions of his actors; how one instinctively understands the play and will require only the gentlest guiding; how another may reveal a total misconception of the part; how another may have a totally different (though none the less valid) interpretation from that envisaged by the director. One actor may reveal an innate slowness of tempo, or too sharp a delivery, that is alien to the part, and so on. Ideally, in a theatre that allows adequate time for rehearsal, the director will work in advance with the principal actors, analyzing and discussing the text. Analysis of the text is as important to the style of a production as psychoanalysis is to an understanding of the characters, and in my opinion ought to come first.

A play as a whole has what Stanislavski termed the 'super objective': the main theme of the play. Each act and each scene has a similar overall objective, like a movement in music. Each scene can be broken down into a number of smaller units, each with its own objective. A unit may be only a few lines in length. If the director breaks down the play in this way it becomes much easier for the actor to digest. Beneath the text of a play there lies the sub-text. The text is like an iceberg, and it is the task of the actor and the director to discover what lies beneath the surface. In any one scene, at any one moment, a character may be *saying* one thing, *doing* something else, *thinking* yet another thought and *feeling* something quite different. In real life we often carry several thoughts and feelings simultaneously. I may be *saying* 'I love you', in what I imagine to be ardent tones, but I may be looking elsewhere than at my beloved, and I may be thinking-feeling:

1 Well, I do love you *but* . . .
2 Not at this particular moment . . .
3 At least, I wish I could get this pipe to light!

4 I wonder if she's going to ask what I was doing yesterday afternoon when she rang and I wasn't in the office.

5 She's looking older tonight—she's getting quite a double chin.

6 Must watch my weight, oughtn't to drink so much beer.

7 Now, why am I saying 'I love you' at this moment?

A whole soliloquy of such thoughts races through our minds at any one second, and my main motive at such a moment may perhaps be something as simple as 'I'm hungry. I wish she'd bring in the supper'; or it may be that behind thought no. 4 lies a more complex motive of guilt. It will be for the director to guide the actor through the complexity of such motives. But no movement on the stage should be made without a motivation for it. There must be a reason for everything an actor does.

The director may choose to take a short scene or unit, block it roughly and then have the actors sit around and read that scene quietly while he chips in with questions and comments, such as—'What do you think she means by that? Don't forget she's tired. It's the end of a long day and it's gone on like this for six months. . . . See what the author says in his description. . . . You'll find the key to this scene on page 20 where X says so and so. . . .' This reading is a kind of open-ended discussion with everyone contributing, even the stage management. The key to a particular problem can come from quite an unexpected source, from the stage manager on the prompt-book to the designer who has been standing at the back watching a rehearsal, or from a fellow actor who has been watching scenes that he is not in. The scene is then rehearsed again, in the light of what has been discussed and discovered, and the blocking may be changed slightly, or even basically, by the actors or by the director. At this stage everything is flexible and exploratory. It is a process of trial and error. Sometimes even the director may not understand a particular scene or it may be that the director or the actors do not yet understand the author's intention.

Once the director feels that he has got a rough shape to a scene he should move on to the next. He cannot solve all the problems at once and must not mind leaving loose ends around. What is aimed at in these early rehearsals is a rough pattern. It is rather like piecing together a jig-saw puzzle. You go for the big bits first—set up the recognizable sections and often, in the process, smaller details will fit into place. Once the actors have got a rough shape to the first act, they can go on to the second and third acts. Having worked on the third act, they are enabled to go back and work on the first act in greater depth. I think it was Rosalyn Tureck who said that you can only play Bach's *Goldberg Variations* when you know what the last note is. In the early rehearsals the actor sees only the trees. Later he is able to see the whole wood.

As basic patterns of movement and business emerge they should become set. Much depends upon the amount of rehearsal time available for the production. If one has a two- or four-month rehearsal period, as is possible in a large subsidized theatre, there is a greater sense of leisure for experimentation. Given only three or four weeks, the director and actors have to learn to stand by what they discover and not keep changing. If the director loses his sense of time and of the progress of work he may find that he has spent too much of the rehearsal period on Acts 1 and 2 and not left sufficient for

Act 3. He has to remember that in the final week he is likely to have less time for the actors, as by then he is having to concentrate upon technical details of lighting, sound and scenic effects.

Sometimes an actor, having found a form for a particular scene, wants to throw it all overboard. It could be that his instinct is right, in which case the director must be prepared to go with him and perhaps re-examine the scene in greater depth. Sometimes, and more often, it is merely that the actor has become bored with that particular scene! Since it poses no more problems for him and seems all too easy, he forgets that it will be fresh for his audience.

In the process of acting an actor arrives at ultimate gestures and inflections and business. This is technique. Having arrived at the external form of a part, he relies upon this to convey the inner core of the play. Even if he is ill, depressed or not at his best, the performance of these moves, gestures and business will move the audience. This is the norm of performance at which the professional aims. Over and above this is the emotional subtlety which, as Stanislavski showed, is bound to vary from night to night. A professional will hope always to give a good performance, but there will be some nights when he gives a better than good performance.

On those occasions when an actor begins to doubt the value of all he has achieved in rehearsal the director must stand firm. I recall one such crisis with an actor who subsequently wrote to me:

'particularly in performance I have learned one big thing. When I was for chucking out some of the movements that we had established, because I thought that they were phoney, and you said, "No, no, keep the shape and then economize and clarify"—how dead right you were! I now feel a terrific shape and form throughout the play on which to rely and within which to strengthen the performance.'

In the early weeks of the production the director needs to probe and prod an actor surgically, remorselessly, bringing him back again and again to the text and the sub-text (the true heart of a play is in its silences), seeking, wooing, demanding the truth of a character rather than the expression of an actor's personal temperament. Of course, the art of directing is also an art of compromise, of diplomacy. The director can probe and prod up to a certain point only, and then, when he comes up against the resistance of an actor's limitations—either as an actor or as a human being—he has to give way, lest he should undermine the actor's confidence. If an actor is sometimes blamed for a performance on which his director has insisted it is equally true to say that a director is often blamed for an interpretation of a part or a scene over which he had no control: this is often the case when the actor in question is a commercial star. I am inclined to think that if, after an initial attempt to achieve truth in performance, such an actor wilfully resists, the director must accept the situation philosophically. He can continue to use all his guile, his charm, his psychology to win a truer and therefore better performance from the actor, but he must be prepared to accept defeat with humour and humility. A director has to work with other human beings whose sense of dedication, in the main, is not even comparable with that of a dancer or a singer. The average actor relies on a minimum of technique, exploiting his personality. Such an actor is concerned less with the interpretation of the play than with the performance of his own rôle and what the critics will say. The director has to strive ceaselessly for perfection and, simultaneously, know when and how to compromise. It is, finally, a matter of instinct. Sometimes, by battling, he may win from an actor a performance that marks in that actor an advance, a growth; at other times he knows that the battling will be in vain, and so does not waste his energies.

There is nothing more exhausting for an actor than to hang around hour after hour, all day even, waiting for his scene to be rehearsed, when with a little foresight on the part of the director he would not have been called until after lunch, or perhaps towards the end of the week. This degree of thought for the actors is rewarded in that they come to rehearsal fresh and eager to work. If the director allots thirty minutes or an hour to a particular scene he should stick to this time and then move on to the next scene. Other directors prefer to plan a day in advance, determining tomorrow's schedule according to the amount of work done today. This will often entail the stage manager telephoning those actors not present to let them have their individual calls for the next day. The director holds the reins of a team of horses that can sometimes become unruly. He has to know when and how to relax the reins, to sense when the actors are tired or have reached a deadlock. At such times there should be space for a giggle, a break for coffee or a drink. The director has to sense when his actors can work long hours and when they are beginning to flag—remembering that it is as easy to over-rehearse as it is to under-rehearse.

The relationship of director and actor is a complex and many-faceted one. Every actor has his own way of working as well as his own problems. It is the director's task to find what method of working will help the actor. He may need to vary his approach to each, especially if he is working with amateurs. A professional is engaged and con-tracted to play a particular part, and he has to get on with it whether he likes the director or not. A professional, even if he is a star, will take notes in public, but the amateur may easily take offence if the director criticizes him in front of others, and perhaps walk out of the production. Therefore the director who works with amateurs has to be much more circumspect and tactful. If he does not know his actors well, or is at all uncertain, it may be advisable to give them individual notes, taking each aside in turn, so that no one can overhear what is said. The disadvantage of this method is that it takes up valuable time, since such individual note-giving often degenerates into con-versations and the rest of the company become restless while waiting to get back into rehearsal. Often the director can vary his method of giving notes. Some he can give to the company as a whole where group scenes are affected; others he can give privately to individual actors. Established actors especially deserve this courtesy. Actors often learn from listening to notes given to others; they may extract points from them which are relevant to the playing of their own particular rôle. This way, notes are often a prelude to valuable discussions and should be encouraged with any company of young or inexperienced actors. Discussion and the sharing of ideas is essential to the atmosphere of a creative rehearsal.

The director ought not to be a dictator. If he is working with not very talented or with inexperienced people, then he may have to organize and dictate moves and business, but, given actors of average talent and intelligence, he should encourage them to be articulate, to participate creatively in the production. A good production is often the result of such collaboration. Yet a play cannot be produced by committee, and if everyone is allowed to chip in all the time and to feel that they are fellow-directors the result is almost always chaotic! A balance must be maintained between the free participation of the actors and the final authority of the director. When necessary, the director should be able to say—'Right, cut the cackle and let's get on with it!'

It often happens that young directors, especially those with a university background, are prone to be over-intellectual in their notes, which at times lengthen into a dissertation upon the play's deeper significance or symbolism. I recall the experience of a young actor who was appearing in a production in London with the Lunts. One morning the director spent an hour with him analyzing his scene while the actor progressively became more and more confused. Eventually Lynn Fontanne, who had been sitting patiently on stage, beckoned to the actor and whispered quietly in his ear, 'What he means is, play it a little faster!'

A director owes it to his actors to be as concise and articulate as possible. If he finds himself becoming verbose or vague he should cease. At a later stage in rehearsal, however, he can often afford to use certain basic phrases which are common usage among actors. Often all that may be required is some such simple note as—

Louder!
More vocal variety!
Too many downward inflections!
I can't hear what you are saying!
Clearer articulation!
You're singing, go for the sense!
Quicker tempo in that scene!
Slow it down!
Not so noisy!
Less energy!
Begin to wind up that scene!
End with a flourish!
Hold the pauses!
You've forgotten what the scene is about!
Find your motivation!
Where would she feel the pain?
Be precise!
You are giving me general emotion, actor's emotion, but I want to know what this
    particular character is feeling at this particular moment!
I don't believe in what you are doing! (This was a favourite phrase of the director
    Leon M. Lion.)
The excitement at this moment means that you will have to tread on cues!
Pitch the voice higher!
You're holding back too much, let yourself go, enjoy this scene!

You're spilling over, over-acting, doing too much, pull it in!
Use one gesture instead of three!
Stop *Acting* it!
You're being too private, too personal, too tele-visual, and I can't hear you!
Enjoy it more! Enjoy it! Enjoy it!

To the outsider these may seem crude recipes, but to the actor who knows and trusts his director they are a kind of shorthand, signposts pointing to a short cut. Often the outsider will be surprised at how little the director may say; but the good director generates an atmosphere within which the actor is able to relax and discover for himself. Each will intuitively sense the thought of the other, so that often in a morning's work the director may not have uttered more than twenty words. Although to the outsider he may seem to be doing nothing, he is, in fact, like a naturalist, watching the actors, observing their processes of work. There is a time for notes and there is a time for silence. Often all that an actor requires is to work on a scene, doing it many times, and in this way resolving the problems of timing, of nuance or stress. The director does not have to justify his presence. Often the mere fact that he is there, alertly watching, is all the stimulus that an actor needs. On the other hand, there will be days when he is in full spate and the actors have to race to keep up with him. He has to veer between being a pilot—especially with experienced actors—and a pioneer who challenges his actors, daring them to make discoveries, to tackle new styles, above all, to experiment!

He should always encourage. Acting is a lonely and difficult exercise. It is very easy for the director, if satisfied with the way an actor is working on his part, to forget to praise him and to devote all his notes to those who are having difficulties. Then the actor goes around tense and worried because nothing has been said to him. Even if the part is small and one for which the actor is perfectly cast, none the less the director must see that he is given some share of the attention and praise.

Yet, while encouraging, he should never be glib. The actor needs to trust his director and to know that he always speaks the truth. I recall working with an actress who got very depressed and said to me, 'I wasn't very good today,' and I replied, 'No, you weren't; but not to worry. It's just that it's an off-day for you.' And the actress, who was very experienced, replied, 'What a relief! If you had said it was all right I should have been much more worried!'

Although the director must not be glib, he does, on occasion, have to risk seeming self-contradictory. Of a certain scene he may say to an actor, 'Good!' and a day or two later reject what the actor found, urging him to experiment afresh. There are occasions when it may be necessary for an actor to shed one reading after another in an attempt to uncover the many layers. The final performance is likely to be the sum of all these readings. Acting, for the actor, is like making a mobile. First, each of the separate parts has to be assembled, and then each part related to the rest, before a perfect balance and proportion is achieved.

Alternatively, there are some plays, especially *avant-garde* plays, when director and actor are together linked in a search for the play's style. Here the actor allows himself to be experimented upon, attempting different ways of playing the part until director and actor sense intuitively that they have found the style necessary for the play, be it by Ionesco, Beckett or Brecht.

• The director has to acquire great patience. If he loses his temper with an actor not only does he upset the others but he may damage the relationship between himself and the actor involved. He can speak sharply, firmly, and indeed must never hesitate to rebuke an actor if necessary. There are occasions when a firm and strong line of attack is what an actor most needs. But whether he wants it or not the director is, for the period of the production, a father-figure to his actors. He must not mind if his actors turn against him, bitch him, are sarcastic or obstructionist. In most cases such attacks are merely the result of a passing mood, a phase motivated by the inevitable tensions that are bound to occur in rehearsal at one point or another. Given any group of individuals working in an intense emotional atmosphere, there is bound to be a clash of temperaments, especially in the case of the actor, who has to work on and through himself, unlike a writer, sculptor, painter or musician, who works through another medium. In the actor's process of imaginative identification with the part he is playing he is less and less himself, as he becomes progressively identified with the emotions and character of another human being. This, in turn, creates an emotional instability and psychological imbalance.

• By many mistakes and blunderings the director will learn to be detached, resilient and patient. The experience of many productions, many crises, begets ultimately a kind of calm and a necessary sense of humour. If he possesses by nature such a temperament, or acquires it over the years, then he will not mind becoming on occasions a scapegoat for his actors' frustrations. Let the actor hate his director for the day but never the play!

A letter from James Roose-Evans to the student cast of *Everyman* at RADA:

My dear cast,

Here, put down as they occur to me, are some of the ideas that I have for our production of *Everyman* which I think may prove very exciting and which should certainly be stimulating for you to work on.

You know that I have set the play in the present day and I want us to find for the play and for each of the characters a modern counterpart. I do not want it to be pious or beautifully elocuted. The play itself has too much vitality, urgency, austerity, crudity, and innate humour —qualities that are to be found in almost all the medieval morality plays. It is a latter day fallacy that religious plays must be performed piously.

Everyman himself is to be seen as a successful young man—we have no indication as to his age but with a young cast it seemed more interesting to interpret the play from your viewpoint. He might have been a boxer, a film star, but I have asked Bryan Stanyon to present him as a pop singer; Adam Faith is his model. Goods is seen as his manager-cum-agent, Beauty is his girl friend, Strength a weight-lifting chum, Discretion his secretary, Five Wits his legal adviser (a seedy, down-at-heel, whisky-fumed Irish lawyer who perhaps tried for the Church originally and got thrown out of the seminary—this would help to explain his smattering of theology). Build up a sense of community. Five Wits, Discretion, etc. are on one level allegorical figures, but in that we judge a man by his friends and associates, I want them to emerge as actual people, not merely types, the friends and associates of Everyman.

Knowledge is being depicted as an Irish St Vincent de Paul nun, a bustling, practical and maternal figure, who probably taught Everyman his catechism. Confession is a Dominican friar and Everyman's parish priest. We have to remember that this is a Catholic play, and that Catholic dogma and practice are woven into the play's fabric. In the background of the production, at Chelmsford Cathedral, we shall see in the chancel the figure of Confession, saying mass, hearing confessions, as well as administering extreme unction to Everyman when the time comes. The purpose of all this is to enable the audience to see Everyman as one of the Faithful, even though lapsed. He is not A Man, but Every Man.

Death—I have had many ideas about this, some influenced by Cocteau—Death on a motor cycle and so forth, but each time I have come back to a quiet, sympathetic yet austere figure in a white raincoat, very still and watchful, rather like M. Henri in Anouilh's *Point of Departure*.

Because of the short rehearsal time available I would like you all to learn your lines as quickly as possible and then to forget them for the first week. In this week I want us to improvise around the characters and situations. Fellowship is Everyman's buddy, his china, and they meet in a bar to talk over drinks. What is their relationship? Is he a singer also? Are they boyhood friends? Then let Bryan, as Everyman, imagine that he has to break the news to him that he has cancer.

Get at the emotions behind each situation. Similarly, when Everyman rings up his manager, Goods, find a comparable situation in which a top artist might suddenly cease to be of use to his manager, who realizes that this boy is about to become a has-been, is fast becoming an embarrassment, a liability.

Get your imaginations working. Accumulate a mass of detail. Talk with each other, have ideas, reject them, try others, until you have a foundation of creative material from which fruitful improvisations can grow. The attempt, each time, is to try to understand the thought and belief of this play as it affects people at all times.

Finally, this is a piece of theatre. It is also a ritual that I want you to make your own. I want to see what you have to offer me and out of all this material we will select, assemble, shape and concentrate the final result . . .

4 The actor and movement

Above all, the actor, and the director, must study people: how they walk, run, sit, stand, stoop, embrace, shake hands, eat, drink, read, smoke, enter a room; use their fingers, hands, wrists, arms, shoulders, backs, torso, legs, feet; how they dress, speak, behave—'Man—be my metaphor.'

The greatest guide here, and little known in England, is François Delsarte, who was born on 11 November 1811 in Solesmes, France. Although he studied to be a singer at the Paris Conservatoire, his voice was ruined through faulty teaching, so that he had to abandon singing as a career. In order that this should not happen to others, he devoted his life to discovering the general principles of human expressiveness and expression. Like the Duke of Meiningen and Constantin Stanislavski, he repudiated the stylistic and pantomimic gestures then in fashion in the world of opera and drama, and set out to discover exactly how real people move and speak in every kind of emotional situation. For many years, long before he began to teach and lecture on the subject, he accumulated facts, observing children at play, alone or with other children or with their mothers. He observed people in different ranks of society. On one occasion he travelled a great distance in order to observe a mine disaster and to study the reactions of the survivors and of the bereaved. He studied the human anatomy, dissected corpses and recorded the behaviour of the insane. Gradually, through all this complex mass of minutiae, he began to detect certain recurring patterns or principles of behaviour, and in 1839 he gave his first lecture in what he called *A Course in Applied Aesthetics*. To his classes came many of the most famous artists of his day, Berlioz, Rachel, Bizet— even MacCready is reported to have visited him. The King of Bavaria sent the leading singers from the State Theatre to be coached by Delsarte. Gautier called him 'the Talma of music'. When he died in 1871, having been showered with honours and degrees in his lifetime, the Cross of the Legion of Honour was placed on his coffin, and in Solesmes a square was named after him. It was Delsarte who defined art as 'the tendency of the fallen soul towards its primitive purity or its final splendour: in one word, it is the search for the eternal type'.

In our own day, apart from Mathias Alexander, who founded the Alexander Technique, no one has achieved so complete a formulation of the principles and laws which govern the use of the human body in relation to space. Delsarte discovered that the body is divided into three zones. That part of the space from the floor up to the lower trunk is the physical plane; that surrounding the upper torso is the emotional plane, while that on a level with the head is the mental and intellectual plane—why else is Hamlet invariably portrayed as leaning his head on his hand? The space above the head is the plane of the super-natural, that which expresses more than the normal, as can be seen from almost any portrait of any saint. Because the body also moves in space, this is further subdivided into three sections: the space in front of the body—the realm of the seeable and the known; the space at the sides, which is more emotional, has a greater sweep; the space behind the body, which has a negative connotation, of pushing something away—behind is the unseeable, the unknown, the subconscious. Delsarte taught that the meaning of a gesture is strongly coloured therefore by that part of the body in which the movement originates and in which it culminates. Every outward manifestation, he claimed, is the result of an inward cause, so that an understanding of the principles which Delsarte codified can help us in our understanding of human behaviour. Let me demonstrate by setting down Delsarte's chart for the positions of the head.

	Head inclined or turned towards object	The Head normal	Head inclined or turned away from object
Head raised and bent backwards	Vulgar familiarity Abandon Intoxication	Ecstasy Prayer to Heaven Exaltation	Strong repulsion or negation
Normal: the head neither raised nor lowered	Favourable criticism	Normal Neutral	Unfavourable criticism
Head lowered and bent downwards	Affection Tenderness	Meditation Inward prayer Grief Dejection	Suspicion

All these positions are naturally modified by whether the eyes are on the object or away from it or closed, by the overall position of the body, by the movement of the limbs and body. The result is innumerable nuances of meaning.

It is interesting, in the light of Delsarte's findings, to read Stanislavski's description of how he arrived at the characterization of Dr Stockman in Ibsen's *An Enemy of the People*. He speaks of Stockman's love for truth and how, with each succeeding scene, Stockman becomes more and more lonely until, at the end, he stands alone on the stage, saying, 'He is strongest who stands alone.' Stanislavski portrayed him as a short-sighted man, blind to human faults, childlike and youthful in movement, laughing and joking with his children and family, the kind of man who brings out the best in other people. Thus, by identifying with Stockman's thoughts and feelings, he intuitively discovered the outward signs of the man: the short-sightedness, the forward stoop of the body, the quick step, the eyes that looked trustingly into the soul of whoever was with him, the index and middle fingers of the hand stretched forward as though to emphasize and drive home his thoughts and feelings to whomever he was speaking. All these details came spontaneously. But where did they come from?

It is at this point that Stanislavski illustrates the magpie nature of the artist.

'Who would ever think [he writes] that I found the make-up and outer image of the rôle of General Krutsky in Ostrovsky's *Enough Stupidity in Every Wise Man* in the general appearance of an old house standing somewhat askew in an older courtyard, and seemingly swollen and overgrown with mossy side-whiskers! From this house ran out little old men in uniforms, with many unnecessary papers and projects *à la* General Krutsky under their arms. All this together brought me in some mysterious way to the make-up of my role in Ostrovsky's comedy. And in the rôle of Stockman also the material for the outer image was taken unconsciously from memories.

'A few years passed and I still played Stockman and little by little I found accidentally the sources of many of the elements of the inner and outer images. For instance, in Berlin, I met a learned man whom I had often met before in a sanatorium near Vienna, and I recognized that I had taken from him the gesture of Stockman's index and middle fingers. Meeting a famous music critic I recognized in him my manner of stamping in one place which I used in my performance of the rôle.' (*My Life in Art*).

In the theatre an actor's gestures can achieve a poetic intensity, the immediacy of an image. Long after the text has faded from memory the remembrance of a particular gesture can vividly restore to us the intensity of a performance. In his book *The Flower in Drama and Glamour*, Stark Young, one of the most cultured critics the theatre has known, describes such a gesture.

'There was a moment in *Oedipus Rex*, [he recalls] as Mounet-Sully descended the Palace steps and lay down flat on the ground. At every performance and on the same word he did that. In that gesture the whole moment was revealed: his body went back again to the bosom of the earth from which it came; he was a part of the doom and motherhood of nature; in him human life returned to its element. Once achieved, that gesture almost departed from any mood that the actor himself might have at any performance of the scene. It had become more important than any mood that he might have. In it Mounet-Sully had discovered something that goes on even now in my mind as the most essential idea and tragic content of that scene. He had found what became the body of the idea, something as inevitable and complete as music.'

In El Greco's portrait of Don Fernando Nino de Guevara (pl 5) the painter has pinpointed the insecurity of the Grand Inquisitor in his portrayal of the hands. While the long tapering fingers of the right hand rest gracefully on the arm of the chair, the left hand clutches the chair rest with rigid, tight control. Further to emphasize this tension, the Cardinal is seated well to the right of his chair, as though retreating from what he sees on his left, the eyes swivelling sharply in this direction from behind his glasses. It is, we observe, the left hand that clutches the chair, and it is from the left that he apprehends some danger or threat. The Latin word for left is *sinister*, and the word carries also the connotation of the unknown, the unconscious, that which is feared because unknown. Thus, behind the smooth, urbane and diplomatic façade of a Spanish ecclesiastic, El Greco has brilliantly conveyed the deep psychological unrest and suppressed violence of this individual as well as of a whole historical movement. The Inquisition, which was at its harshest in Spain and used to try secular crimes as well, acted habitually on the principle that it was better that ninety-nine good Catholics should be tortured and sometimes burnt rather than that one heretic should escape. It is this atmosphere of fear and suppression that El Greco has caught superbly in the look of the eyes, the position of the body in the chair and the tension of the hands.

As Regan in *King Lear*, Gwen Ffrangcon-Davies had a recurring gesture of the left hand, a flexing, folding and unfolding movement rather like the automatic gesture that some women make towards the back of their head to tuck in and tidy loose wisps of hair. She played Regan, not like the Queen in Snow White—a frequent interpretation —but as a cosy, homely, sexy lady. This soft, feline movement of the hand had the reassuring familiarity of a cat rhythmically washing a paw; but when it came to the blinding of Gloucester, this cat's paw suddenly showed its claws. As she said, with swift sadistic pleasure, 'Put out his eyes!' so this hand shot out in a sharp incisive movement. At that moment one saw, beneath the exterior of the domestic cat, the atavistic, pre-datory quality of the wild cat.

Tyrone Guthrie has described Tore Segelke, the Norwegian actress, as giving the finest interpretation in our time of the part of Nora in Ibsen's *A Doll's House*, and in 1956, when she gave a one-woman recital in New York, she included the Accounts scene from this play. Seated at a table, facing her husband, she spoke in a low voice, almost a monotone, with hardly any emotion in the voice.

'We have been married eight years. Does it not strike you that this is the first time we two, you and I, man and wife, have talked together seriously?'

One hand clenched the arm of the chair on which she sat, while the other held firmly on to the table. In Tore Segelke's performance it was the tension in these hands, the whitened knuckles, that revealed to us the depths of emotion. We knew that if this Nora were, for one moment, to relax her grip, she would break down and cry, revert-ing to the tearfulness of the doll-wife from which she was now turning. It was a per-formance of extraordinary economy.

In the Moscow Art Theatre production of *Uncle Vanya*, the actor playing the title rôle had a recurring gesture of languidly lifting one soft, white hand and running it through his long hair. It was a gesture that completely expressed the languor, boredom, culture, dreams and restlessness of Vanya. One recalled the words of Stanislavski— 'From that time on Uncle Vanya became for us a cultured, soft, elegant, poetic, fine type of man, almost like the unforgettable and enchanting Tchaikovsky.'

The American designer Robert Edmund Jones, recalling his first impressions of Nijinsky, for whose ballet *Til Eulenspiegel* he designed the sets and costumes, observed that throughout their conversation Nijinsky scratched at the skin of his thumbs, which were raw and bleeding from this compulsive habit. It was this detail which conveyed, more than anything else, the impression of a highly charged dynamo, a machine over-wound and likely to snap at any moment.

When Sir James Barrie, an excessively shy and withdrawn little man, used to shake hands, he would carefully restore the person's hand as if to say, 'Thank you, but now you keep it. I don't want to come any closer!'

So it is that the more habitually we observe the gestures, mannerisms and movement habits of other people, the more we appreciate the words of a pioneer like Delsarte:

'Gesture is more than speech. It is not what we say that persuades, but the manner of saying it. Speech is inferior to gesture because it corresponds to the phenomena of the mind. Gesture is the agent of the heart. It is the spirit of which speech is merely the letter . . . The most powerful of all gestures is that which affects the spectator without his knowing it.'

5 The actor and improvisation

Often when an actor gets stuck and doesn't know what to do with his body and the words sound stiff and awkward and there is no feeling of life to the scene, all that the director may need to do is to remind the actor of *the given circumstances* of the scene. Certain key questions about the part he is playing will serve to stimulate the imagination of the actor.

Who are you?
Where are you?
Why are you here?
Where did you come from?
Where are you going?
How did you come here? (on foot, by bus, by car, etc.)
When is it? (what time of hour, day, month, year)
What kind of weather is it?
Whom are you expecting to meet?
What are you expecting to find?

The character an actor is required to play may perhaps be a schoolmaster, and the actor or the director will go on to probe:

What kind of schoolmaster? What subjects does he teach? Is he old-fashioned in his methods of teaching or progressive and experimental?
Does he enjoy teaching or is it merely a means of earning money?
Did he once enjoy teaching and, if so, what has happened to make him no longer enjoy it?
Did he always want to be a teacher or is this merely a second, perhaps even a third choice?
Is he a frustrated artist or writer?
How successful is he? Is he popular? If so, why? If not, why not?
Is he married? What is his relationship with his wife? with his friends? (has he any?) with his colleagues, the boys, the principal?
How does he employ his spare time? Has he any hobbies? Has he any hidden virtues or vices? What are his day-dreams and fantasies? Has he any eccentricities?
What are his personal idiosyncracies, gestures, habits, mannerisms, growing out of all this?
How does he dress? How does he walk? What are his hands like? How does he speak—has he an accent? Is it genuine or acquired? If acquired, how and why? Where was he born and brought up? What kind of childhood did he have? What kind of parents, grandparents and family life?

No part can be successful unless the actor believes in it, and in order to achieve this he has to be *imaginatively involved*. Because the author does not give the actor everything he needs to know about the play the actor has to ask himself these questions.

Nowadays the general concept of truthfulness in performance is more widely accepted and the present generation of actors is prepared to improvise and explore, to feel the way into a part, layer by layer and detail by detail. However, what one often sees is not realism as Stanislavski would have recognized it, but naturalism. In the third act of *The Seagull* the actress playing Madame Arkadina may be very naturalistic in the way she eats her meal while talking with her brother Peter Sorin, but she will only achieve *realism* when we see her eating not only in character (in spite of her vanity and sensitivity about age is she not perhaps greedy and self-indulgent?) but also in the mood of that particular moment. Thus the way she eats will be not merely naturalistic but, as in real life, it will reveal to us, if we are observant, something of her inner conflicts and agitations and preoccupations *at that particular moment*. It is the tensing of a facial muscle, a shadowing in the eyes, a hesitation in the speech, a nervous movement of the feet that reveal to us another human being. Such half-tones, inflections, gradations, undercurrents, according to mood and thought and impulse, according to text and sub-text, shifting and changing often with bewildering rapidity, go to make up that intricate graph of a human heart.

It will be realized how important is the practice of observation, of keeping a mental, or even an actual, notebook. We know, or think we know, how *we* behave, but the actor has to know how *other* people behave. This is one reason why acting has such a therapeutic value in any community. The study, rehearsal and performance of a play deepens our understanding and awareness of other people. Our thinking becomes less self-enclosed.

Most actors, like most people, tend to be self-absorbed. It is for the director to remind his actors how other people behave in differing circumstances. If an actor is playing an old man he needs to be aware of the movement and behaviour patterns of old people, how they walk, sit, eat, how they react under sudden pressures. He will need to know the difference between an arthritic old person and one who is suffering from high blood pressure. It is only on the basis of careful and detailed observation that an actor can begin to build up the character and characteristics of the *particular* old man he is called upon to play, remembering that any one man is a composite of all that has gone before —'the child is father to the man'. We tend to see more clearly in an older person the characteristics of the child that once was.

Sometimes it may help to get the actors to rehearse in conditions similar to those in the play. Once, rehearsing *A Midsummer Night's Dream* with students of the Royal Academy of Dramatic Art, I took them all on a trip to Epping Forest and there blind-folded the actors who were playing the four lovers and set them running; while those who were portraying Oberon, Puck, Titania and the fairies climbed trees or practised camouflage, learning to merge with the landscape, becoming branches of trees or rocks or part of the undergrowth. The 'lovers' tore their clothes, banged into trees, slithered down muddy banks, lost their tempers and got very annoyed—which is exactly what would happen to Demetrius and Lysander, Hermia and Helena! We know from the text that the seasons are topsy-turvy and that, although the flowers of summer are in bloom, there is also snow on the ground and the fields are flooded with mud and there are heavy mists and fogs. There is no light from either the moon or the stars, so that in the heart of the forest it will be as dark as in a pine wood.

Always one must relate to reality. When I was rehearsing *Under Milk Wood* I used to take my casts to spend an evening at the Welsh pub in Grays Inn Road so that they might observe how Welsh people sing. The Welsh have a unique way of singing in pubs that is quite unlike the slurred thumpety-thump-roll-out-the-barrel manner of the English. The Welsh *care* about singing. It is in their blood. As often as not one of the men will jump up on the bar and start to conduct. One observes how groups of men, their arms linked around the shoulders of one another, will lean in towards each other, forehead to forehead, not looking at each other but turned in, tuned in as it were, to the song, concentrating on the note, the pitch, the harmony and the melody. When Dylan Thomas was in New York rehearsing for the first performance of *Under Milk Wood* he was violently ill, vomiting and retching. After a while he opened his eyes and said sadly, 'Tonight in my home the men have their arms around one another and they are singing.'

Although each member of the cast of *Under Milk Wood* that played at the Lyric Theatre, Hammersmith had been in one or other of my productions of the play, many of them met for the first time a week before the opening. In order to help them arrive at a familiarity with one another within the intimacy of the production, I set the whole cast a group improvisation. They were to imagine themselves attending the funeral of Mr Waldo: Mr Waldo being the small town's lecher, 'rabbit-catcher, barber, herbalist, cat-doctor, quack'. He is 'the black spit of the chapel fold . . . the old ram-rod', described in Thomas's poem *Lament*. For an hour and a half the cast improvised: arriving at chapel, the notices given out by the elders, the Bible read, hymns sung and then the actor playing the Rev. Eli Jenkins preached an extempore sermon lasting twenty minutes which most movingly expressed the spirit of the play as well as the essential philosophy of Thomas himself. He took as his theme the words of his evening prayer.

Improvisation is one of many methods available to a director and is not an end in itself. Outside a permanent company it is a technique that must be used with discretion. If it tenses an actor or further inhibits him it should not be employed. It has two chief values: to involve the actor more imaginatively in the given circumstances of a scene and to develop the sense of ensemble playing.

There are many exercises in improvisation which an actor can use in his training, but in the rehearsal of a play there are basically three kinds of improvisation which a director may employ. The first is a general improvisation based upon physical conditions. When Joan Littlewood was rehearsing *The Quare Fellow*, a play about prison life, she had the cast marching up and down on the roof of the theatre and carrying out various exercises that helped to give them the feeling of being prisoners, subject to routines, monotony, supervision, deprived of privacy, always under surveillance.

If actors are having difficulty with a scene the director may suggest that they improvise it in their own words. Given the characters they are, the circumstances of the play and freed from the text, they will be forced into a closer, more spontaneous identification which can have a very releasing effect, enabling them to discover what was previously inhibiting them. Joan Littlewood often withholds the text of the play in the early stages of rehearsal and gets the actors to improvise scenes similar to or taken from those in the text.

Alternatively, the director may suggest to the actors that they improvise a scene which is not in the play. I recall rehearsing Barrie's *The Admirable Crichton* and getting

1–3 *The Admirable Crichton*, Sir James Barrie. Acts I, II and III. Pitlochry Festival 1960.

C

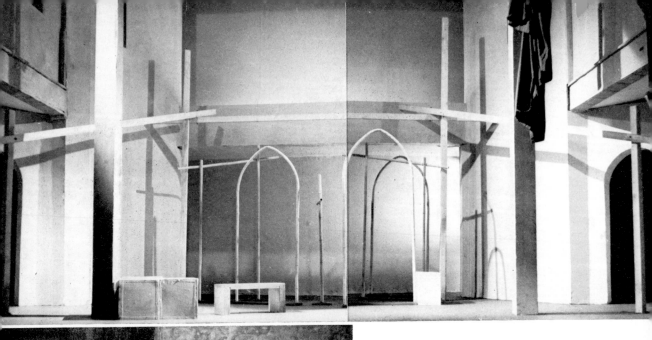

4 *The Marriage of Saint Francis*, Henri Gheon

5 Don Fernando Nino de Guevara by El Greco

6 *Opposite:*
Director's lighting sketches for *Cider with Rosie*, Laurie
Lee

7–15 *Cider with Rosie*

8 Model set for opening scene   9 *Below:* Chairs become sheaves of corn, a table top the wagon

10 The kitchen setting

11 *Below:* The chairs become a charabanc

12 The table becomes a bed

13 *Below:* The roundabout at Weston-super-Mare

14 A winter hedge at sunset

15 *Opposite:*
Hywel Jones as the young Laurie Lee and Narissa Knights as Rosie

16 *Napoleon in Love*, R. F. Delderfield. The shadow device is here employed to conceal a difficult scene change.

17, 18 *Below and opposite:*
Nathan and Tabileth, Barry Bermange. A large piece of white silk suggested in turn the bridal gown, bed linen and shroud of an old Jewish couple. Robert Bernal and June Jago, Edinburgh Festival 1967.

19 *Nathan and Tabileth*. Backlighting throws a scene into silhouette.

20 *The Two Character Play*, Tennessee Williams. Mary Ure and Peter Wyngarde

21–26 *Opposite:*
Letters from an Eastern Front.
A documentary piece of theatre created by James Roose-Evans, based on the last letters of the men of the German Sixth Battalion at Stalingrad and the letters of the children in Hiroshima at the time of the H bomb.

21 A pyramidical rostrum suggested the Hill X on which the main fighting took place . . .   22 trenches . . .

23 tent hospital . . .

24 *Below:* Christmas mass . . .

25 heap of bodies in Auschwitz . . .   26 *Below:* Hiroshima—a child emerges from a burning pagoda.

27 Bridget Turner as Masha in *The Seagull*
by Anton Chekhov

Opposite:
29 Martha Graham in her ballet *Frontier*
30 *Les Forains*, Roland Petit

28 David Hemmings in *Adventures in the Skin Trade*
by Dylan Thomas

31, 32 *Circus Boy*, Michael Redgrave. A more striking effect was achieved by abandoning the original idea of back projection.

33 Doré engraving *Farinata degli Uberti* for Dante's *Inferno*

34 Director's sketch for *Paradise Lost* inspired by the Doré engraving

D

35 A fifteenth-century French illuminated manuscript   36 An Angami warrior's topknot
Such diverse sources provided ideas for the halo for God the Father in *Paradise Lost*.

37 Director's sketch
38 'and with swift wings explores his solitary flight . . .'

39 Nicholas Chagrin and Madeline Bellamy in *The Little Clay Cart*. Requiring a minimum of properties and a maximum of mime, King Sudraka's 1500-year-old Indian classic is a superb challenge to an imaginative director.

40, 41
Murder in the Cathedral, T. S. Eliot. Director's sketch and actual performance. Bryan Bailey as Thomas à Becket and Terry Wale as Fourth Tempter. Belgrade Theatre, Coventry.

42–49
David Garrick's adaption of *The Taming of the Shrew* given a very individualistic treatment. Set within the context of a dream, it shows a mixture of Commedia dell' Arte, Mexican and Spanish influences. Pitlochry Festival Company 1960.

50 Loie Fuller in *Danse du Lys*

51, 53, 54 (*overleaf*):
Loie Fuller's costume was the inspiration for
Aphrodite's billowing robe in this production of
Euripides' *Hippolytus*.

52 Loie Fuller, lithograph by Toulouse-Lautrec

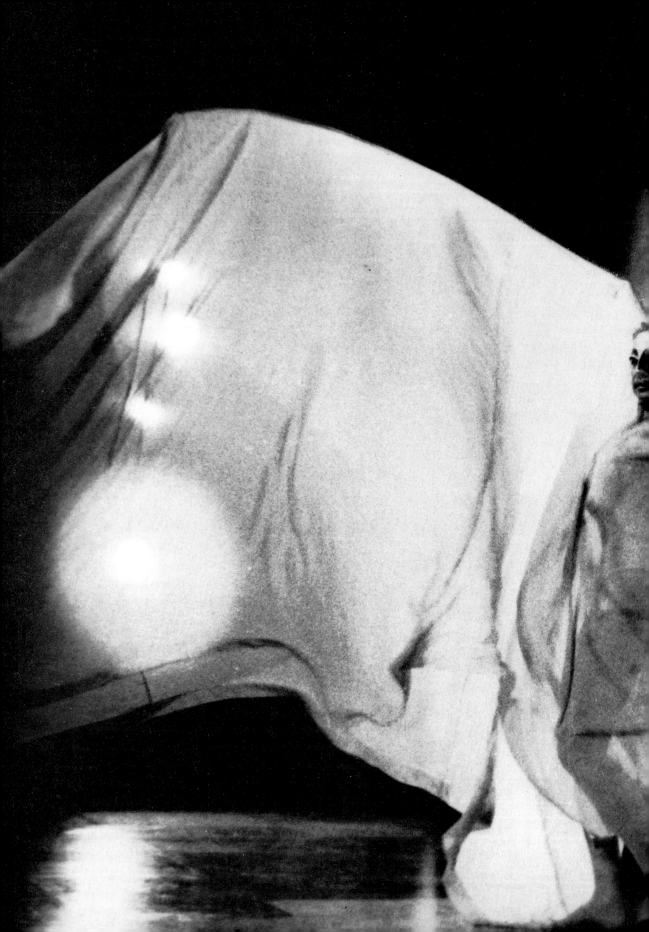

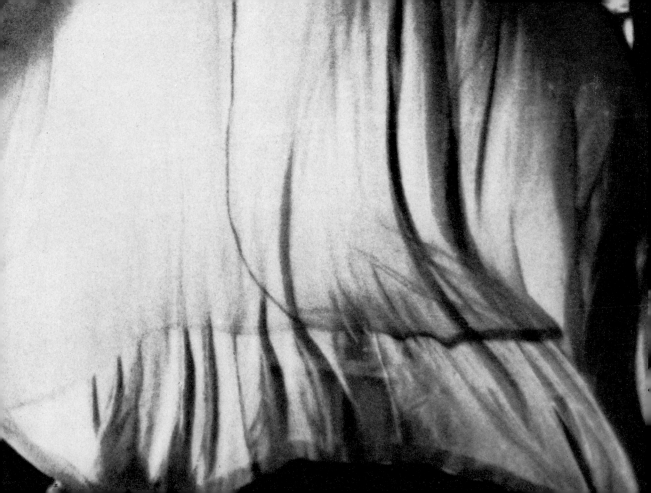

55–59 Euripides' *Hippolytus*. A length of white silk used by the chorus variously suggested their common veil, washing, the sails of a ship, embroidery and the dramatic re-enaction of the voyage of Queen Phaedra.

Chorus: Yoma Sasburgh, Louanne Richards, Jessica Barnes; Phaedra, Betty McDowall; Nurse, Norah Blaney.

the cast to improvise being shipwrecked on a desert island, the experience that happens to the characters between Acts 1 and 2. Gradually the actors re-created the atmosphere of distress, of being soaked to the skin and their elegant clothes ruined, their fear of strange insects and animals, the sense of their complete helplessness when faced with an alien situation for which they are totally unequipped; only Crichton, assisted by Mr Treherne, sets about building a shelter for the night.

At one point Tweeny spotted a ship and they all started to shout, growing more and more possessed and hysterical as the ship passed on. This incident in the improvisation sprang from a reference by Tweeny in the third act when she refers to their seeing a ship pass the island. 'How we all ran like crazy folk to the water and screamed and held out our arms. But it sailed away and we've never seen another.' The emotion possessing the actors at that moment in the improvisation, the violent and unrestrained shouting and screaming, fading into the silence of despair and desolation, was one that the actors never forgot, and it coloured the way they shouted off-stage at the end of the third act when another ship is sighted which does see their signals and returns them to civilization. In the silence Lady Mary suggested that Mr Treherne, being a clergyman, say a prayer. Night was falling. It was growing chilly. Quietly, in the background, Crichton was lighting a fire. Crichton the practical. All together they said the Lord's Prayer, sang the hymn *Abide with me*, then feeling comforted they gathered around Crichton's fire, nervous of the vast openness of the night, the sky, the sea and unknown land all around them. Gradually they all fell asleep, leaving only Crichton and Mr Treherne discussing the programme for the next day. It was after this improvisation that one of the actors articulated the feelings of the rest—'For the first time I really felt I was a member of that family!'

Although actors can improvise upon general situations and make up imaginary characters, they cannot improvise upon an existing text until they have carefully studied the play and its background. Then they should be able to improvise for an hour or more a scene in the play or one outside the text. Without such detailed preparation the exercise is likely to fizzle out in ten minutes. As an example of the kind of research necessary here are notes made on the character of Masha as she appears in the first act of *The Seagull*. When I am directing a play I make similar studies of each of the characters, a case history as it were, gleaning from the text every possible clue. The director is then able to consider in more detail the problems of each of his actors. He has to get inside the skin of each rôle. And it is from such a detailed study of the *whole* play that the actor draws his material for an improvisation.

MASHA aged 22, the daughter of Shamrayev and Pauline. Rural and agricultural background, with smatterings of theatricalism. Father reasonably well off? Wears black. Why? Says dramatically she is in mourning for her life. By wearing black she denies her own femininity and youth, identifying herself with the elderly and widows. She therefore looks older than her age. In Act 2 she says: 'I drag my life like an endless train. Very often I don't want to go on living at all.' She makes an effort to pull herself together and shake it all off by marrying the impoverished schoolmaster, Medvyedenko. She is touched by his fidelity, but cannot care for him. She is in love with Konstantin and only married Medvyedenko because it will remove her from the proximity of Konstantin.

Though she has a baby, she reveals little maternal concern and eventually spends more and more time away from home and at her parents', near Konstantin, especially once she has learned that Nina has gone off with Trigorin and had a baby by him.

She is silent all through Konstantin's play in Act I until Arkadina starts calling for her son. At once she rises, saying, 'I'll go and look for him. Kostya, coo-ee!' Konstantin's comment later on is, 'Masha's looking for me all over the park, what a nuisance she is!'

When Masha finds him and says, 'You'd better go indoors, your mother's waiting for you,' it is surely Masha who is worried? Arkadina will have forgotten by now. Is it not probable that it is Arkadina who is playing the piano indoors at the end of the Act?

When Konstantin runs off after Nina, 'violently' rejecting Masha in front of the doctor who murmurs sympathetically, 'Youth! Youth!' Masha replies caustically, 'When people have nothing better to say, they say Youth! Youth!' and then takes snuff.

1 Masha is jealous of Nina.
2 Masha is distressed for Konstantin because his play was not a success.
3 She is irritated by Medvyedenko's attentions. It is not merely the weather that is close at the beginning of the act but Medvyedenko who is dogging her.
4 She is humiliated at having to inflict on herself the torture and self-abasement of offering, like a servant, to go and look for Konstantin.
  Almost unconsciously she invokes Konstantin's wrath, yet it is better to be noticed than ignored when you are hopelessly in love and know that it can never be reciprocated.
5 She is angry at being humiliated in front of the doctor (her mother's former lover) by Konstantin whom she loves.
6 She is jealous that Dorn should offer sympathy to Konstantin. Is she not young also and deserving of sympathy?

She is deprived by the doctor of her drug—he has thrown her snuff-box away, commenting, 'Disgusting habit!' He says, 'We'd better go in,' but IN is what she cannot stand, the trap of the house, the household and all its tensions. Suddenly her compulsion to speak to someone breaks through her inhibitions and reserves and she replies, 'Please, wait a moment! I'd like to tell you (i.e. I want to confess)—I—I—wanted to before. I must talk to someone.' . . . 'agitatedly' in Chekov's stage direction at this point.

It is at this point that we get Masha's father-fixation.

1 'I dislike my father . . .' Instinctively, in the presence of her mother's lover, she identifies with her mother and her mother's complaints about Shamrayev in Act 2. She knows that her mother loves Dorn and has known him as an escape from the monotony of life on the estate and the insensitivity of her father.
2 'But I am very fond of you. I don't know why, I have a strong feeling that you're very close to me (in an early version of the play Chekov made Masha the illegitimate child of Pauline and the doctor but removed this as unsubtle) . . . so, please help me or I shall do something silly. I shall make a mess of my life, I shall ruin it . . .'

At this point Masha breaks down, crying, 'Oh, I can't go on like this!' and the theme of loneliness is again repeated. 'No one, no one knows how wretched I am! 'and Doctor

Dorn, the father-lover figure, is linked with the image of Konstantin as lover, when in Chekov's stage directions: *Masha puts her head on the doctor's chest and at last admits, 'I love Konstantin.'*

Improvisations performed by individual actors will vary considerably in quality according to the imaginative freedom of each actor. There are some actors who just cannot improvise and who have to be given everything by their author and director, gesture by gesture, inflection by inflection. It is only by experience that the director learns to know his actors. Given a cast of young actors, however, he should not hesitate to get them to improvise.

Within a group improvisation especially, it is easier for the less imaginative to participate. The actor who cannot think of anything to say or do and who feels stuck out on a limb when called upon to improvise on his own will often find himself caught up in the group awareness and responding to a lead given by someone else. This way he often surprises himself. If an actor loses his concentration he should not drop out or become a spectator but stay within the improvisation, maintaining a relaxed concentration, keeping in character, until something occurs to him, precipitated by the others or prompted from within himself. Not to break one's concentration, not to give up at such a moment, is an important creative principle and will serve an actor in good stead on those days when he is tempted to say, 'I don't feel like rehearsing that again.' Almost invariably, unless the actor is patently exhausted or unwell, the director should insist. It is when an actor's conscious work on a part seems to have failed or to have reached an impasse and he is in despair that his subconscious takes over and quite suddenly the problem resolves itself, often in an unexpected manner.

6 Working with props

If the play is a naturalistic one I think it is essential to have at rehearsal as many of the props and pieces of furniture as possible. Where furniture is hired it may be necessary to use substitute furniture in rehearsal, but, whenever the budget permits, those pieces of furniture that are going to be used a great deal by the actors should be hired in advance. The actors have to build relationships not only with one another as the characters in the play but also with the furniture and objects in a room. Objects and possessions acquire associations of their own and, as in real life, people relate to an environment, to the sights, smells and sounds around them. While the imaginative actor can visualize much for himself, none the less the subtleties of a performance, as well as the accuracy of timing, can only grow out of rehearsing with the actual objects and furniture to be used in the production. In this way he can also anticipate some of the physical problems. If he has business with paper Christmas decorations he will learn how easily these tear if roughly handled; if he has to write in chalk on a blackboard he will discover how a long piece of chalk is liable to snap in two, as well as how long it will take him to write, and this in turn will affect the timing of his own dialogue or that of another actor. If, as in Barry Bermange's play *Oldenberg*, the actors have to furnish an empty room and then smash and remove everything, tearing down the wallpaper and painting slogans on the walls, it may be necessary to have a mock-up of the set, working with all the furniture and props from the very first rehearsal. One should regard the furniture and properties in a production as other characters in the play. The actual blocking of a scene will often grow out of the actor's relationship with the physical objects around him. Such a way of working has the added advantage of removing much of the usual strain experienced by actors and stage management at dress rehearsals when, so often, they are confronted for the first time with furniture that is different from what they have imagined or that proves too heavy or too awkward for certain business. It means that at the very first dress rehearsal the actors will feel much more at home, and therefore relaxed, on the set; especially if at rehearsal the stage manager has also repeatedly reminded them of the physical nature of the set, the positioning of steps, rostrum, which side and which way a door or a window opens.

A director cannot foresee everything that is likely to occur in a production, but if he has provided the props and furniture, then he has provided the actors with the means whereby they can grow into the reality of the play and so discover further business. I recall two such incidents when rehearsing Dylan Thomas's *Adventures in the Skin Trade*, adapted for the theatre by Andrew Sinclair. The part of the hero Sam Bennet, a portrait of the young Dylan, was played by David Hemmings (pl 28), while that of George Ring, a camp young man, was played by Doug Fisher. In the scene set in Mr Allingham's junk shop, among many props used from the start was an old-fashioned gramophone with a large red horn. Throughout rehearsals the actors were encouraged to improvise and experiment. I suggested to Doug Fisher that he unclip the horn and use it as a telescope through which to peer at Sam; that he perch in it as on a chamber pot; blare into it like a megaphone and then, as he and Sam began to recite poetry, Sam put it on his head like a coolie's hat. Finally, both pretended to be old men, the one shouting into the horn as the other held it to his ear like an ear-trumpet. In this way the use of the horn became not only a visual joke in a Dylanesque manner but it also showed the two characters discovering and sharing a common vein of fantasy and inventiveness; yet none of this business could have been discovered if the actors had not been able to rehearse with the props.

Later in the same scene Sam Bennet shouts, 'I want out!' and Mr Allingham, thinking he is referring to the toilet, picks up a toilet roll and flings it across the room to Sam, who throws it to George, who throws it back to Mr Allingham. What one was after here was not merely a piece of comic business but a moment of visual calligraphy. By holding on to the loose end and aiming the roll upwards the paper shot out, curving through the air. As it was hurled backwards and forwards, so for a moment the stage was full of streamers, curving and crossing in flight like rockets in the sky, then falling to impede momentarily and comically the actors' progress. It is by rehearsing with the props that business evolves, and simultaneously one discovers the problems inherent in perfecting any piece of business. Even something as simple as pouring out tea, eating a meal, lighting a cigar (less easy than a cigarette) requires patient rehearsal. If an actor has to light a cigar in the middle of a speech he will have to find a place where a pause will hold, otherwise there will be an uncomfortable silence while the audience waits for the cigar to light. It may be that such a pause will serve to emphasize an awkward moment in the scene. In a comedy, however, it may hold up the flow of the action, in which case the actor will need to light the cigar on a laugh line, on someone else's line or at the beginning of a speech.

In the third act of Oscar Wilde's *An Ideal Husband* Lady Markby, accompanied by Mrs Cheveley, calls on Lady Chiltern and tea is served. With the wit and sparkle of this conversation piece, it is essential that the ritual of tea should not dominate the scene but merely enhance it. The footman, under the supervision of Mason the butler, will set the table, bring in the tray of tea-things and place the tiered 'curate' with its plates of sandwiches, cakes and small biscuits. It will remain for the butler to serve the tea, which Lady Chiltern will pour. The butler will proffer both milk and sugar to each of the guests, serving from stage left. Only by patient rehearsal with the props can the detail of such a scene be resolved. Since the butler will place only one cup of tea at a time on his salver, he will have to make a number of journeys from the tea-table to each of the ladies. On the first journey he will hand the cup of tea and proffer milk; on the second he will offer the sugar bowl, while finally he will offer food. He will make three such journeys to Lady Markby and three again to Mrs Cheveley. It will be found necessary for one of the ladies to refuse both sugar and food, and since Mrs Cheveley would be very conscious of her figure, it is in keeping with her character that she should be the one to decline. Lady Markby may accept a small sandwich, an asparagus tip rolled in delicate bread and butter, but she will not have time to eat it—she is far too busy talking! In fact, the whole elaborate tea will return to the kitchens practically untouched. Meals were in general a great deal more elaborate in those days, and we know from Laurie Lee's mother that at that period the ladies never did more than peck at their food:

'Why not?'
'—Oh, it wasn't thought proper.'

In this example from *An Ideal Husband* there are three stages observable. The business of serving tea is indicated in the text; the director has to do research in order to find out what would be provided and how the tea would be served; finally, he has to take the reality and, selecting aspects of it, provide the audience with a vignette of social manners at that period and, in addition, so time the business that it serves to highlight certain moments in the dialogue.

Just as it is important for the actors to rehearse with the props and furniture, so it is important for them to be aware of their costumes, since, especially in a period play, these may well dictate their movements and physical behaviour. In the case of a period play the women should wear practice skirts and, where necessary, corsets at rehearsal. It does not matter if they look odd. What is important is that they should be able to imagine themselves in costumes, say of the 1890s, with their elaborate corsetings and coiffures. If at the opening of the second act of *The Seagull* the actresses remember this, and that it is also midday and the height of summer, they will soon realize the value of stillness at the beginning of this scene, of lying in a hammock, sitting in the shade of a tree or a parasol. In the first act of *An Ideal Husband* the ladies will have very long trains to their dresses, and it will be advisable for the actresses to rehearse with a length of material the same as that of the trains so that the moves may be correspondingly placed and other actors avoid treading on the trains. In addition, the actresses will then be able to allow for the timing and the business of adjusting the train when they rise or turn. Such things at that period were done most gracefully, and the actresses have to acquire a similar ease without looking down or in any way drawing the audience's attention to their manipulation of yards of material. Similarly, the actress has to learn how to subside into a chair so that the dress spreads itself evenly, and under no circumstances, if she is meant to be a well-bred lady, should she fuss with the dress or attempt to adjust it when seated. The head is upright and poised, and what happens below is as graceful as a swan in sail lifting or readjusting its feathers. At the same time it would be very dull if all the actors were to move as though they were performing a minuet!

In a naturalistic play not one detail must be overlooked by the director. If a kettle or saucepan is seen standing on a hot plate the audience will expect to see it steaming or boiling. If someone enters a room and we know that he has been out on the moors on a winter's day we shall expect to see mud on his boots. We shall expect the characters in a play to wear clothes suitable to their social status, their particular occupation at that moment, the time of year and the kind of weather, and above all to the kind of people they are. If we are shown the same set in the next act, after an imagined lapse of several months or even longer, we shall expect to notice some changes in the room. If in the first act it was winter and in the second it is summer not only will the quality of light be different but there may be flowers or fruit or vegetables appropriate to the time of year; newspapers and magazines changed or rearranged; coats and hats hung behind a door are likely to be different or in different positions; furniture and objects moved around; a coal scuttle in a slightly different position; slippers now shoved under the table. The director's eye for such detail stimulates not only the imagination of the actor but also that of the spectator.

7 *The director and the stage management*

To rehearse in the manner that I have described presupposes a company having its own theatre or rehearsal room where furniture and props can be stored, as well as a conscientious team of stage managers and an efficient company manager. The latter is responsible for the smooth running of the whole production from first rehearsal to final performance. He must know the requirements of the director and the designer and have been in at the early production conferences. He must know the budget for the production and see that this is not exceeded. He will collaborate closely with the designer, accompanying him on visits to the scene dock to check progress on the construction of the set. Once the model of the set has been approved by the director, it is general practice that he does not go back on any essential part of it. In an experimental theatre or workshop this rule does not necessarily apply, since, very often, the set grows with the production; this was the practice of Joan Littlewood and her resident designer, John Bury. In a theatre that has to work to deadlines, as in a repertory theatre, alteration causes delays in construction and adds to the overall budget. If, however, the director does want to alter some feature of the set he may be able to anticipate this change before work has commenced on it by visiting the scene dock with the designer.

One of the secrets of running a theatre successfully lies in wise expenditure. The budget of a production must be worked out in detail in advance, and once agreed upon, whether it is £5, £500 or £5000 (c. $12.00, $1200.00 or $12,000.00), must be strictly adhered to. The budget, therefore, may often determine the style of a production, even sometimes the choice of play.

The company manager will delegate various tasks to the stage managers and assistant stage managers under him, some to find and purchase various props or effects, others to visit museums or libraries to check the detail or authenticity of certain props. He will be given a weekly float of money for stage management purchases, and he will keep all bills and will account to the management for the expenditure. It is his job to order necessary equipment, fix appointments for the actors with costumiers or wig-makers. The secret of a successful company manager lies in his ability to plan the production in advance. In the professional theatre he is often responsible for paying the actors, collecting their insurance cards, looking after their hotel reservations when on tour, and in the West End, once a play has opened he is in charge of the production, taking regular understudy rehearsals, watching the performance each night and giving basic notes. If in a long run the director has not been in for a while it is for him to telephone the director if he feels that the production is slipping. Often during a long run it will be necessary for the director to give the actors notes and to call occasional rehearsals. This serves to stimulate the actors afresh.

One of the stage managers will be appointed by the company manager to be on the book. This means that this stage manager is not only the prompter but is responsible for seeing that everything is ready for rehearsals. At the first rehearsal the stage manager, checking with the ground plan, will either chalk out the dimensions of the set or use lengths of white tape attached to the floor by drawing pins or coloured sticky tape. It is the stage manager's job to see that all the furniture is set out ready for the rehearsal, having first checked with the director the positioning of the furniture and marked these positions on the ground plan. All this will necessitate the stage management arriving half an hour before rehearsals commence so that the actors and director do not have to stand around waiting for the stage to be got ready.

The prompt copy is more than the text of the play from which an actor is prompted. It is the book of the whole production. On the right-hand side is the text, while the facing page is a blank sheet on which are recorded all the sound, lighting and tab cues, as well as movements for the actors, relating to that page of the text. The prompt copy will also contain details of the arrangement of furniture in each scene, the disposition of props on the set, and what personal props are required by each actor in each act. Props should always be checked by a stage manager before the show; if they are heavy, awkward or large they will be placed, in sequence of use, on the prop table in the wings, the props for each act being clearly marked. Small personal props, such as cigarette cases, lighters, spectacles, gloves, walking sticks, etc., will be given to the actor, and it is for a stage manager to check individually with each actor 'at the half', before the performance begins.

In the front of the prompt copy there should be a list of the names, addresses and telephone numbers of the entire company, actors, author, designer, director and stage management. Duplicate copies of this should be typed and given to each member of the company. Where the director is working with amateurs there should also be included the telephone number of the actor's place of work, his employer permitting. Often rehearsal schedules have to be changed or unexpected costume or wig fittings are required, and it is important to be able to contact the artists as soon as possible.

In the early stages of rehearsal, while the actors are working with their scripts, the prompter is busy writing in the moves and business being evolved by the director and actors. He, or she, will at first write these in pencil, since they may be changed from day to day before being finalized. It is important that the prompter be able to tell an actor where he was yesterday at any one moment in a scene: 'On that line you move downstage and sit at the kitchen table and drink your coffee. As you sit Monica moves across to the sink and starts washing up.' In the prompt copy all moves and business will be written in ink once finalized, while all lighting cues will be in one colour, and all sound cues in another. This enables the prompter to see ahead at a glance when lighting or sound cues are coming up. Each of these will have a warning cue, inserted two or three pages ahead, and the prompter will whisper on the inter-com system, 'Stand by LX cue 21!' and then, when it comes up, will announce, 'Go LX cue 21!' Similarly with sound cues and tab cues. If the cueing is done by a lights system he (or she) will press red for 'stand by!' and green for 'go!'

The stage manager is technically running the show during the performance and has to liaise between the company manager, the director, the actors and the other stage managers. Although occasionally he will depute someone else to be on the book in rehearsal, so as to familiarize another with the running of the show in case he should be ill, he will be present at every rehearsal and, apart from the director, is the one person who will know most about the running of that show. As a prompter he will come to know in rehearsal where there are intended pauses, and these will be marked on the actual page of the text by the symbol ⓟ. He will come to anticipate an actor's needs in rehearsal. A good prompter is a rare but valuable friend. It requires absolute concentration, never going into a daydream, keeping a finger on the text, following it word by word, so that the moment an actor dries the necessary word, phrase or line can be given *at once*. If an actor dries, it is no good fumbling or saying, 'I'm sorry!' and then looking for the place. By that time the actor is likely to have remembered or been prompted by a fellow actor or by the director. If the prompter is dozy, slow or does not speak up (a frequent failing) so that the actor is obliged to ask, 'What did you say?' then the actors are likely to become tetchy. Apart from the emotional upheaval caused by identification with a part, the actor, in trying to remember his lines, moves and business, as well as reacting to his fellow actors, is often under considerable strain. Therefore an efficient, clearly spoken, swift, off-the-mark prompter can do much to establish a sense of security in rehearsal. The only time the prompter may legitimately fail, and then the actor ought to be patient in his turn, is when at the same moment that the actor dries the prompter is trying to write in a new move! Every actor has different needs, and the prompter will soon learn which actor does not want to be prompted unless he asks for it. Sometimes it breaks a particular actor's concentration to be prompted and he prefers to paraphrase in order to keep the scene going and later, during a break in rehearsal, he will check with the prompter where he went wrong. Another actor, however, may be helpless without the author's text and require constant prompting. But the prompter cannot really win, because actors are often contrary creatures and quite likely to alter their requirements!

Personally I prefer not to have actors prompted in performance. Such a prompt is invariably heard by the audience and breaks the spell. If the actors have been rehearsed in the proper way they should be able to get themselves out of any difficulties without the audience knowing or being aware that anything has gone wrong. However, older actors are often uneasy if there is not someone standing by ready to prompt them. It is a recurring nightmare of many actors that they are on stage playing Hamlet and suddenly cannot remember a word. If the majority of the cast are happy not to be prompted in performance but one actor does wish to be should the need arise, it will be for the director to instruct the stage manager to prompt only this particular actor.

It is important for the prompter to check that the actor is speaking the author's text and not merely a paraphrase. Much depends upon the quality of the writing, but with authors like Beckett, Coward, Pinter and Shaw every word, every pause has been carefully weighed and balanced before being committed to paper. Each of these authors has an acute ear for what works in the theatre. Actors are great ones for cutting a play in the early stages of rehearsal and being loth to have anything cut later on! Much depends upon the skill and experience of the actor, but all too often he cuts what he initially finds difficult. In this case it may be necessary for the director to persuade the actor to try to get inside the character more, to explain to him carefully the author's intention. I think that one ought always to try to give the author the benefit of the doubt. A speech may not seem to work at first but prove to do so after a week or more in rehearsal. A very gifted leading player, of course, especially in comedy, may choose to rewrite considerably, and almost invariably the instinct of such a performer is correct and these rewrites will be absorbed into the final text. If in the final weeks of rehearsal the author and director feel that the play will be better served by certain cuts, then this should be done. The cuts should then be rehearsed so that the actors can re-orientate their performances. Finally, in the professional theatre it is important that the prompt copy be kept up to date. In the event of a new actor taking over a part, or of the play being revived at a later stage, it will be essential to have a detailed and clearly legible record of the production.

Move notation—a suggested shorthand for the stage manager's prompt copy

X	cross
CS	centre stage
DS	downstage (towards audience)
US	upstage (away from audience)
USL	upstage left
USR	upstage right
DSL	downstage left
DSR	downstage right
↗	move on a diagonal USL
↖	move on a diagonal USR
↙	move on a diagonal DSR
↘	move on a diagonal DSL
Ⓟ	pause
↻	circle
←	straight across stage, left to right
→	straight across stage, right to left
(Table) (Sofa)	indicating pattern of movements
	go upstairs
	come downstairs
	pace up and down
S	sit
R	rise
K	kneel

8 Lighting and sound effects

Although the lighting and the sound effects in a production are often left until the end, they can and should be planned in advance. In a naturalistic play it is simply a matter of thinking what sounds would be the most likely in such-a-room-in-such-a-place-at-such-a-period-and-at-such-a-time-of-year, and deciding at what point in the text such effects should be heard. The stage management can then make up a working tape of all the effects in sequence to be used in rehearsal. They ought not to be introduced, however, until the actors not only know their words but are beginning to relax into the play. The actors will then become familiar with the effects. It can be very alarming for an actor at the dress rehearsal to hear for the first time all sorts of sound effects, usually coming in on the wrong cue or at the wrong volume, since they have been left so late; he is likely, and justifiably, to ask somewhat tetchily, 'Is that going to come in there?'

When a scene requires continuous music in the background, as in the case of a party or a dance, the director will not know in advance how long the scene is likely to play and may need to delay ordering such effects until he is able to time the scene. With other effects he will be able to gauge more accurately, by their use in rehearsal, where they add to the effectiveness of a scene and where they merely distract. Naturalistic effects must be used consistently and throughout a production. If in a scene the text refers to a particular sound effect, as in the first act of Chekov's *Ivanov* when one of the characters says, 'Listen to that owl!' it would be as distracting to an audience to bring in that one sound effect on cue as it would be to have too many effects. In this case, if there are owls in the vicinity, then we should hear them intermittently throughout the scene. If a certain effect is meant to be continuous, whether it is a storm or traffic, this should fluctuate in intensity and not be merely the same band of sound repeated over and over! Once a continuous sound effect has registered with an audience it can be taken down in volume or faded in and out at intervals, occurring during pauses in the dialogue—although the director must take care to fade in the sound several lines before the pause. If a particular effect, however logical it may be in terms of the action, continues to worry the actors, then it should be cut; likewise if a sound effect is not immediately recognizable to an audience for what it is meant to be.

The level of volume required for each cue, and this may vary during the actual effect, can be gauged only roughly in rehearsal. It is not until the scenery is up and the speakers are in position that the levels can be fixed, since the set will to some extent muffle the speakers. According to the direction from which the sound is meant to be coming, there should be separate speakers under individual controls. In a stylized or experimental production the director may even have speakers out front, or used stereophonically all round the auditorium. During the dress rehearsal these levels will have to be checked again in relation to the actors, while at the public dress rehearsals the director may have to make final readjustments. In large commercial theatres there is the additional problem that what is heard by the audience in the stalls is not always the same as what is heard by the audience upstairs. Because sound travels upwards the acoustics in the stalls, especially when they are below the level of the stage, are often less good than in the dress circle, the upper circle and the gallery; also, since the back of the stalls is usually under a low shelf formed by the dress circle above, the sound is further muffled in that part of the auditorium. All this means that if the sound effects are exactly right for the stalls they are likely to prove too loud and distracting for the audience upstairs, in which case the director will have to make a compromise. What is important is that he should check not only the sight lines and audibility of the actors from every level and seat in the auditorium but also the sound levels. In a theatre that is unfamiliar to him he ought always to check on the acoustics, either with the management or with actors who have played there before. In some theatres the actors will have to use a great deal of vocal projection, and they ought to be warned about this well in advance so that they can adjust their performances accordingly.

On the master tape, and there ought always to be a spare one standing by in case of accidents, each cue will be clearly marked and will have a lead-in. This prevents one cue accidentally running on into another. If at the dress rehearsals the sound cues are not coming in with the precision to which everyone has become accustomed at rehearsal, this is probably due to the fact that the prompter is now solely on the book and having to signal the cues for effects to other stage management; in consequence, there may well be a fractional pause between the giving of the cue and before the stage manager on the tape-deck switches on the tape or the electrician starts operating his dimmer board. Much depends upon the individual temperament. If the person on sound or LX is slow on his reflex actions, then it is probably best to anticipate the cues by one or two words. In this case, once the show has opened and the sound technician or electrician has grown familiar with it and begins to speed up, it may be necessary to revert to the original cues. By keeping an eye on the show after it has opened, the director can adjust these things.

The lighting of a production should be planned well ahead. The electrician or lighting consultant should read the play, see the model of the set and also be in at all the early conferences. The director will discuss with him the kind of lighting he wants and will indicate on the ground plan the main acting areas in each scene so that the electrician can decide where he will set his lamps. As soon as the director is clear where he wants his lighting cues these should be written in to the electrician's copy. If there are a lot of effects required it may be advisable to prepare a series of sketches for the electrician. When I was directing Laurie Lee's *Cider with Rosie* I prepared a notebook of water-colour sketches for the lighting consultant, Richard Pilbrow (pl 6). Even if a director does not know how to light a show himself he should be able to say what kind of lighting he wants. About two-thirds of the way through rehearsal, or as soon as there is a run-through of the play, the electrician will want to come and watch the production so that he can make his own notes.

Once the set has been erected the electrician will need to set his lamps, and this can take a whole day. However, in order to give the stage management and designer more time to work on the set, dressing it, marking on the stage cloth the positions of the furniture, preparing the prop table (while the actors rehearse elsewhere), the electrician may choose to work through the night with one or two ASMs on hand to assist him. The set-up, as it is called, must be done independently of the actors, who will only get in the way of the stage management. The director will consult with the company manager as to when the latter considers the set will be ready for the actors to rehearse on.

When the director comes to light the production, a task that takes several hours and may go on all night, he will have at least one ASM to stand in for the actors, moving about the set so that he can check the lighting. Since standing about for a long period like this is more tiring than might be imagined, once the director has seen that a certain position needs more light, a lamp re-angling, or a different coloured gel inserted, he should tell the ASM to relax until the electrician is ready to recheck that position. Where the director has planned a very choreographic production or an elaborate lighting plot, it may be better to light with the actors.

Ideally the director and the lighting consultant should sit out front to light a show so that they can judge the effects, and the lighting consultant will call out to the electrician, who is operating the board, the numbers of the lamps that he wants brought up or taken down and at what levels—as with sound, levels are always numbered from 1 to 10 in quarters, $\frac{1}{4}$, $\frac{1}{2}$, $\frac{3}{4}$, full. I think it is a useful exercise before lighting to have all the lamps switched on one after the other. Not only does this show the director the different angles and sources of each light but he may discover that one or more give a special effect which he can utilize. He will then note these particular lamps.

Lamps are hung in three main positions. FOH (Front of House), *perches* (vertically on either side of the proscenium arch), *booms* (vertically on either side of the stage) and *spot-bars*. These are suspended above the stage and are numbered from down-stage upstage so that the first spot-bar nearest the audience is spot-bar No. 1 and so on. All lamps are numbered from stage left to stage right. *Floats* (footlights) are rarely used nowadays or, if at all, on a very low check, since they throw shadows on the back wall of the set. In addition to these positions there will be a number of lamps on *stands*, either *spots*, open *floods* or *pageants*. These will provide wing lighting or backing to windows and doors. They can be fixed close to the floor or at any height required. At the back of the stage there may be a sky-cloth or solid *cyclorama* wall used for sky effects. This will be lit at the bottom by a *ground-row* (similar to the floats) and overhead by *battens*. On to the cyclorama, or back-projected if it is a *scrim* (a gauze screen), there can be projected special moving effects, or static projections painted on slides.

Once the lighting plot has been established, and each cue will have its own time sequence according to how fast or slow the lights are meant to come up or fade, the timing of the cues must be given by the director, and can vary from a count of three seconds to a slow build-up over three or more minutes, or a fast fade to blackout (FBO), or a snap DBO (dead blackout). It will then take the electricians two or three rehearsals to get the sequence of cues running smoothly, dependent upon the kind of equipment and staff available. It is at this stage of rehearsals, however, that the director must exercise great patience. Everything always takes so much longer than he expects, and he may be inclined to get impatient and shout out, 'What are we waiting for?' He must not develop a persecution mania and feel that the stage staff are setting out to be ob-structionist or are planning to sabotage the production, but realize that the technical side of a production always takes much longer, has to be properly rehearsed and cannot be unduly hurried. If there is time, this is where a special technical rehearsal should be called when the technical staff can run the tab cues, sound and LX cues in sequence and rehearse the scene changes.

Within a naturalistic play much use can be made of atmospheric lighting so long as key scenes are clearly lit. At the opening of *The Seagull* the sun is setting, and because the scene is set under tall trees, down by the lake, once the sun has set the stage will be in shadow except for the afterglow of the sunset. Not until the moon rises, during Konstantin's play, will the stage be clearly lit. Atmospheric lighting must be used sparingly and skilfully. If the audience halfway back have to strain their eyes, peering through the gloom to see the actors, then the director has underlit the play. He must check the lighting from different parts of the theatre. When an actor is meant to be in a dim light he will need to use more projection and clearer articulation when speaking. The audience always experience some difficulty in hearing an actor when they cannot see his face clearly. Strong, clear lighting is for this reason essential to comedy, since the facial reactions and double-takes of the actors are as important to laughs as the timing of lines and business. A dim light has a muted effect both on the audience and on the actors. Unless, as in *Thark* or *The Cat and the Canary*, a comedy or a farce has scenes that are spooky in character, masses of light cheers an audience and stimulates the actors as though they were promenading in the sun on the Riviera! Often, quite unconsciously, actors are affected by the stage lighting and if a scene which worked in rehearsal seems to be 'down', it may well be that the director has underlit it, just as a sensitive and intimate scene can be marred by overlighting.

Much variety can be achieved within a scene by the use of lighting, and this can be effected in two ways. The first is barely discernible to the audience and is comparable to the use of highlighting in painting. It consists of a number of small cues within the general lighting of a scene. If the actors are playing a scene in one corner of the stage and the action then shifts to another area the director can check down the lights very slightly on the first group and bring up more light on the next group in such a way as to focus the audience's attention without their being aware of what is happening. Of course there may be occasions when the director wants the audience to notice, in which case the lighting cues will happen more swiftly or be more dramatic in effect. Highlighting can be subtle, as in a Constable, or startling, as in a Tiepolo or Fuseli. Indeed, a young director will learn much about grouping and lighting from a study of classical painting. Alternatively, he can provide visual variety within a scene by emphasizing the natural sources of light within the action. In real life a cloud crosses the sun and momentarily the room is darkened; the sky darkens before rain, turns green before snow, while the reflective surface of snow or flooded fields throws up a stronger, clearer light. A character entering a room at night may switch on or off a table, standard or overhead light; open or close the curtains; leave a door into another room ajar so that light comes through. Even the time of day will be marked by a different direction, as well as quality, of light. In a variety of ways, according to the logicality of such action within the text and the imagination of the director, the lighting can heighten the atmosphere of a scene, set the mood beforehand, shift our attention and keep the set alive rather than dully flooded with light. However brilliant the design of a set, it will not come alive until it has been lit, which is why in America most designers insist on lighting their own sets.

A director ought to guard against the temptation of the cyclorama. It is very tempting to set the action against the cyc. and to flood it with light but, if used too extensively, it will have a deadening effect upon the spectator. The eye becomes dazzled by the large area of luminosity, and the actors in front always seem less well lit. The effect is similar to seeing people bathing in the sea on a sunlit day when they appear bronzed and black against the dazzle of light reflected on the sea's surface. If a bare cyclorama is used it should be for certain scenes only, unless it is the director's intention in a particular production to dehumanize the actors, making them seem like statues set against the sky. Otherwise the cyclorama should be broken by the outline of the set or by very skilful lighting so that it does not dominate the action and dwarf the actors.

At all times the lighting must serve the play. Ultimately it is a combination of imagination and artifice—as well as of accident—that results in a well-lit production. When lighting, a stage hand may knock over a lamp on the floor, bang a ladder on to a lamp overhead and swivel its position, set a lamp swinging, switch on the working light—accidents that may suddenly achieve a startling or beautiful effect which could never have been anticipated and which the director then absorbs into the production.

To stage a production means serving the playwright with a devotion that makes you love his work. It means finding the spiritual mood that was the poet's at the play's conception and during its writing, the living source and stream which must arouse the spectator, and of which even the author is sometimes unaware. It means realizing the corporal through the spiritual. It is a way of dealing with a work, with the places and properties necessary to the setting, with the performers, with the poet who has conceived it, and, finally, with the audience for which it is destined. Charged with the interests of this audience, the director must unite the stage and the auditorium, the spectacle and the spectators. He must organize that area where the active players on the stage and the passive players in the auditorium meet each other, where the spectators penetrate and identify themselves with the action on the stage, and where the actors satisfy their need to prove and free themselves by reflection in the people who listen and look on.

Jean Giraudoux modestly says that the playwright does not make his play, that the audience makes it out of the elements furnished by the playwright. 'The audience,' he declares, 'hears and composes as it pleases, following its own imagination and feelings.' He compares a dramatic work to a piece of pottery painted in false colours, whose true colours and finished design do not appear until after it is fired. A play receives the finishing process of an ordeal by fire through contact with an audience.

LOUIS JOUVET

9 *The last few days*

There comes a point in rehearsal at a run-through when, without scenery or costumes, the play suddenly fuses into a whole; the actors catch fire from one another and they experience a sense of unity, feeling at last on top of the play. This is an important occasion, signalling to the director and actors alike that the play and the production are working. This unity often disappears in the final week of dress rehearsals as the actors take time to relate to and integrate with the set, the lighting, costumes and effects. However, the director should not despair. This is only a phase, during which he should not worry the actors unduly; as much as anything they are now wanting an audience. Many small problems will resolve themselves in performance. A production needs to play itself in—a fact of which few critics are aware. At this stage before the first performance the actors are very subject to nerves and tension; the director must be patient, encouraging and positive in his approach, even if privately he is in despair. Technically too these last days are a strain for everyone, and much depends upon the overall control of the company manager. If he has planned well in advance and organized his stage management team so that every member knows exactly what he or she has to do, then the actors will have less cause for anxiety.

In this final week the director has to marshal together the component parts—lighting, sound, film, scene changes, effects, business—fusing them into a whole. During this period the director concentrates less on the finer points of acting than on the hundred and one technical points: the positioning of a lamp, a late lighting cue or too quick a fade; a music cue too loud, or too soon; a piece of furniture wrongly set; someone's make-up to be toned down as a result of the colour gels used in a particular scene; a prop missing; a wrong detail of costume or someone who can't do his quick-change in time ('Right, let's rehearse that several times!'); a wig that has to be re-dressed; a corner of the set that has a light leak and must be canvassed; a note to actors not to bang dressing-room doors and not to talk during performance; a blue bulb to be rigged for the prompt; a voice on tape still not synchronized with the images on the screen; the projector breaks down and a specialist has to be brought in; or a special rehearsal has to be called for a very complicated technical sequence.

Whenever possible, a production should have, as an absolute minimum, two public dress rehearsals; only one, especially of a comedy, can have disastrous consequences upon the first night, since the first time a cast plays with an audience out front is a time of discovery and excitement. Such a performance tends to go well and then, on the following night, there is a slump. If it is possible to have only one public dress rehearsal it would be better to open cold, in which case it will be necessary before the second performance of the play to call the company for a rehearsal of at least the first act, if a complete run-through cannot be arranged. This helps to limber up the actors.

The director should never give notes during or immediately after a performance when an actor is in no state to receive them. Once the performance commences the actor is on his own and has to be trusted. Notes should always be given the following day. Even if the first performance has gone disastrously, or been marred by some technical fault, the director should not appear backstage with a face of doom. If it has gone badly the actors will need no telling. At such a moment they will need

F

encouragement and warmth and laughter. The director, like any good actor, has to learn to hide his own feelings on occasion!

The final testing of a play and a production is with an audience. However rewarding the rehearsal period, it is the performance of the play before an assembled company of people towards which all have been moving. The director, who will continue to visit and watch the production, giving notes and rehearsing whenever necessary, will learn much from watching people during a performance. Those moments where an audience fidgets, coughs, looks to see the time, reads the programme, slumps, dozes, are often symptoms of what is not yet right with a play, with the production or an actor's performance. With an *avant-garde* play or experimental production it is possible that the audience are not 'with it', in which case it is they who are at fault rather than the play or the production. To each generation there comes an author like Beckett or Pinter or Ionesco who, initially, bewilders and even angers or alienates the public. The music of Stravinsky, the dance works of Martha Graham, the paintings of Picasso, the theatre of Samuel Beckett have each in turn been derided by critics, booed by audiences, and later understood, cheered and acclaimed. But in general it will repay the director to examine clinically the reaction of the audience. He will discover that certain business does not work, fails to get a laugh or takes too long; that one scene needs cutting and another perhaps played with a quicker tempo or more emphasis, and correspondingly he will adapt the production.

It is often all too easy, in rehearsal, for a director to forget those who are coming to see the play. He must keep trying to gauge the impact that it will make upon them. He is the play's first spectator, its most critical and its most appreciative. Yet, because he knows the text intimately and, sitting in an empty theatre, can hear even the quietest scenes, he may forget that the presence of an audience can muffle and blanket the resonance of a building. Seated in the stalls, hugely enjoying himself, he can all too easily forget the audience seated at the back or high up in the gods, the elderly or the deaf. All too often, although quite unconsciously, he is sitting where the critics will sit, directing the play to and for them. But a play does not exist for critics. A play exists for an audience that has paid to be entertained, moved, excited, disturbed.

10 The director as magpie

To be a successful director requires a certain attitude of mind. Like any creative artist, a director has to gather and hoard, in magpie fashion, an extraordinary, often haphazard, amount of material. A detail observed, an experience recollected, will suddenly rise to the surface and help to illuminate a scene with which an actor is having difficulty, decide the atmosphere of a set or the arrangement of furniture within it, or stimulate the director with ideas for a new production. At times the mind of a creative artist resembles one of those attics which are used not only for storing apples in winter but pieces of old, often unwanted, furniture, bundles of books, folders of drawings, trunks full of letters and fading photographs, childless toys, empty garments, broken instruments, dried flowers, useless objects: a clutter of many decades, centuries even. Yet each and every one is waiting to be brought to life by the creative imagination.

A director may have many lumber rooms in the attics of his memory, and although periodically he may tidy, sort, arrange and file their contents for future reference, there must always be a certain amount of untidiness, of clutter, for this is essential to the creative process. Because of the fallibility of one's memory, however, it is advisable to try to file material under the appropriate headings and, when reading, to underline with a pencil key passages, making notes in the margin or on the fly-leaf. It can be helpful to keep a journal, jotting down impressions of things seen or overheard, pieces of music, scraps of conversation, sketches of people's hands or some detail of their dress, ideas for sets or productions. It is useful also to keep a general scrapbook containing photographs of people's faces, objects, rooms, houses or articles, cut from journals and newspapers.

For instance, if I open the file marked '*Circus*' I will find pictures, cuttings, jottings accumulated over the years. First there is a photograph of the Roland Petit company in *Les Forains*, which was the first ballet I ever saw, in 1954, at the Adelphi Theatre, London. The ballet showed a group of strolling players setting up their booth, putting on their costumes, and as soon as a crowd has gathered, commencing their performance. As the hat is passed around and the crowd disperses rapidly, the players are suddenly tired and disillusioned. Sadly they pack up their belongings, dismantle the booth and trundle everything away on their cart. The choreography by Petit, the music by Sauguet, the décor and costumes by Christian Berard portrayed sharply the gaiety and the sadness of circus life. It is for the set, however, that I preserved this picture (pl 30). Against black drapes, on a bare stage, two white ropes are looped to suggest the outlines of a circus tent, suggesting also the tight-rope of the trapeze artists, as well as being a symbol of the tight-rope of their existence which these wandering players traverse. Similar lengths of white rope were also employed by Martha Graham in one of her earliest dance works, *Frontier* (pl 29) to suggest the vast plains and horizons of pioneering America. Similarly, for Leonid Adreyev's play *The Life of Man*, Stanislavski designed a set made of white ropes against a background of black velvet drapes. Like lines in a drawing done on black paper, the ropes marked the contours of the room, the windows, doors, tables, chairs. From behind these lines of rope the actors seemed to materialize as out of an endless darkness.

Next in the Circus file comes a child's toy circus, bought for sixpence from Woolworth's and made of thin cardboard. Opened up, it shows the silhouettes of people standing outside a circus tent. Opening back the flaps of the tent, as on an inner stage, we see inside the circus ring and the raked audience. At once, on the principle of Shakespeare's forestage and inner stage, it suggests a simple way of staging a play about circus life. From geographical magazines come pictures of famous artistes, as well as samples of circus posters and lettering. There are books such as *A Seat at the Circus* by Anthony Hippisley-Coxe and *Spinners of the Big Top* by Pamela Macgregor-Morris, which provide one with information on traditional music, the order of presentation in the ring, technical terms, etc. Other items in this file include photographs of dancers and circus performers, rehearsing not in their glamorous costumes but in long woollen tights and sweaters. There are various reproductions of Picasso's studies of circus folk, of paintings by Renoir, Toulouse-Lautrec, Dame Laura Knight, Steven Spurrier; a pop-up circus book bought at a reduced rate on Coventry Station platform; photographs of the famous clown, Grock; a Russian circus doll bought in New York; a wooden Polish clown; recordings of big top music; and notes and poems and stories about circuses.

But always when one is reading, walking, observing, facts have a way of sticking like burrs caught on a country walk, lodging themselves for future reference. Everything is stored away for future use, reappearing spontaneously when needed. Instinctively the artist observes, absorbs and then, at a later stage, recollects. For instance, in Lytton Strachey's biography of Queen Victoria we have glimpses of royal evenings, the dull exchange of platitudes, looking through books of engravings laid out on a round table (a detail that I found of use as an activity for Lady Chiltern with two of her guests in the first act of *An Ideal Husband*), while in a corner Prince Albert and three attendants would play game after game of double chess. Similarly, we have a fascinating and revealing glimpse of the newly-wedded Victoria hurrying down the long corridors of Windsor, trying to keep up with the long-legged stride of her beloved Albert.

Such historical facts can illuminate a performance, and I have never forgotten three moments in Joan Cross's performance as Queen Elizabeth in Benjamin Britten's opera, *Gloriana*. On her first entrance she appeared as though climbing uphill and out of breath. Suddenly she hauled herself up by holding on to the halberds of two lines of soldiers. At once we glimpsed the frailty of the ageing Queen and saw how, instinctively, she could convert this into an oblique flirting with her troops. In another scene, alone and bald, without her wig, she lifted state documents close to her eyes in order to read them. In a later scene, at a state function, she joined in the dancing of a galliard with animal-like shouts of pleasure. Suddenly she stopped, out of breath, her heart troubling her. One was reminded of those contemporary documents which record how in her last years Elizabeth the First showed renewed signs of that feverish love of amusement which had been more becoming in her youth. In 1602, just before her death, she was still reported dancing, but Sir John Harington observed that 'she doth now bear show of human infirmitie'.

When I came to direct André Obey's *Frost at Midnight*, a play which is set in a medieval corn-market, I covered the floor of the stage with straw, thereby adapting a detail I had stored up in my memory from the account of Paul Hentzner, a German visiting London in 1598, who was presented to Queen Elizabeth at Greenwich. 'We were admitted by an order from the Lord Chamberlain into the presence chamber, hung with rich tapestry, and the floor, after the English fashion strewed with hay.'

As a boy there were certain books in our home that made a vivid impression on me. One of these was Gustave Doré's illustrations to Dante's *Inferno*. These fearsome studies of souls in torment would fascinate me, and when I came to stage Milton's *Paradise Lost* there was one engraving in particular that I recalled. It is that of Dante and Virgil standing aloof and smug in the obscurity of the surrounding darkness, gazing down at the tormented body of Farinata degli Uberti, who stands in his grave, the tombstone uplifted, with smoke and fire issuing from below. Pondering how to stage the first appearance of Lucifer—

> At once as farr as Angels Kenn he views
> The dismal situation waste and wilde;
> A dungeon horrible, on all sides round
> As one great Furnace flam'd . . . .
>   torture without end
> Still urges, and a fiery Deluge, fed
> With ever-burning sulfur unconsum'd . . .

I recalled this engraving by Doré and had Lucifer discovered standing in a trap, so that his chest was level with the floor of the stage, lit from below and smoke rising, his great antlered wings silhouetted against the trembling reds and oranges of the cyclorama (pls 33, 34).

In the same production the costume for God the Father was taken from a fifteenth-century illuminated French manuscript, one of the *Très Riches Heures de Jean de Berry* which shows God the Father in a long-flowing robe of blue, with white hair and beard, and an ornate halo of gold. The actual construction of the halo was solved by a photograph taken from a geographical magazine which depicted princes of the tribe of Angami warriors wearing sun-burst crowns, made from splints of bamboo sewn to a circlet of light wood and attached to the back of the head (pls 35, 36).

About two years before I did this production, or had even thought of staging Milton's dramatic poem, I visited the interdenominational chapel at the Massachusetts Institute of Technology, designed by Eero Saarinen, and it was the altar screen there that provided the idea for the gates of Paradise. The chapel is a round brick structure, a squat tower centred in a moat. Inside, the brick walls undulate, and from concealed apertures in the floor the reflection of the water in the moat outside ripples its patterns of light across the surface of the walls. Three broad circular steps ascend to a rectangular marble altar behind which, suspended from the domed ceiling, is a screen made of segments of gold attached to a curtain of fine wire. It hangs in mid-space, and from a circular, honeycombed aperture in the roof the sunlight descends, causing the oblongs of gold to flash like the tongues of fire at Pentecost.

This suspended screen was re-created for the stage by means of hundreds of oblong shapes cut from sheets of shiny gold, bronze and copper-coloured wrapping paper, attached to lengths of black thread, weighted at the bottom with pellets, and flown in and out as required. It took three days to make but cost only one pound for materials!

For the scene depicting Lucifer flying through the seas of Chaos—'and with swift wings explores his solitary flight'—I had the stage covered with enormous areas of black velvet. Underneath were actors, some of whom manipulated the material, some held gas-filled balloons on nylon threads, while others handled mobile spotlights. Lucifer lay on his chest, quite static, poised on an upright pillar, his legs in the air and his wings sweeping backwards, as though he were swooping down. Only the actors under the material moved slowly up and down. The lurid lighting, the trailing smoke, the balloons like planets and the mass of black material like an oily sea, marvellously evoked the poet's description (pl 38).

In one sense there is nothing new. Like a magpie, the creative artist gathers and stores up for his future use. What is original is his use of these things. Martha Graham may use movements influenced by the Eastern dance, but it is in the way she employs them, and what she uses them to say, that make them uniquely her own. Similarly, Saarinen's chapel at Boston is an original, a re-creation of the image, 'a mighty fortress is our God', whereas the pastiche of Yale remains an example of plagiarism. Only when the artist has absorbed what he has observed can he later recollect it and transmute it.

The process of observing is a continuous, often subconscious, activity. Lying in bed in hospital you may notice in the bed opposite another man being shaved. Just above his head and sitting astride of the partition is a young Negro holding the step-ladder for another Negro who is cleaning the domed lamp-shades on the ceiling. Here is action on three levels, and the young Negro in the centre links the upper and lower level, his hands holding the steps for his mate above, while he gazes down watching the barber shave the prostrate man. All too often in the theatre directors move their actors about in upright positions like partners in a ballroom.

On a summer's afternoon in a small Welsh village you may hear two children, squatting in the street, playing a toy xylophone, or throwing pebbles at a telegraph pole and counting up to ten in Welsh, *un, dau, tri, pedwar, pump*, etc., and both these details are stored up and later remembered when you are directing a play like *Under Milk Wood*. Wherever you go you are quietly recording details of colour, shade, texture, pattern, light, sound, rhythm, smells, atmosphere. It might seem obvious that a director should automatically record such minutiae of reality, and yet, time and again, one sees plays staged by directors of reputation without reference to the environment of the story or the situation. Yet this was one of several lessons to be learned from the Moscow Art Theatre on their various visits to London. In the second act of their production of *The Three Sisters*, while Masha and Vershinin are seated late at night quietly talking, one can hear in the dining-room beyond the quiet chink of cutlery being laid out, while one of the servants tunes and strums his guitar. Occasionally, an old beam creaks. Outside the wind howls, while far away in an attic the old nurse can be heard crooning a lullaby. Thus the scene is carefully composed of a texture of sounds, not obtrusive but selected and orchestrated into the text, woven into the fabric, giving us the extra dimensions of the other rooms in the house and the different activities of that hour of night, the countryside and the weather outside. Merely to record naturalistic sound effects is not enough, since, more often than not, this would merely distract the attention of the spectator. What is required is a carefully composed score. Just as in a poem, key images have to be selected and then disposed and arranged to form a perfect balance, so in the theatre the detail of reality is there only to emphasize and heighten certain moments.

Faced with any scene, a director has but to switch on a mental tape-recorder, open one of the many doors of his imagination and thereby look out on an orchard in Russia in the early morning, on to a tiny village in Wales or listen to the sounds late at night in an old house when almost everyone has retired to bed. In the first act of *The Seagull* we know from the text that the air is close, that there may be a storm and that because the sun has set it is damp. Of course, one must guard against taking everything that is said as the literal truth. When Masha says, 'My, how close it is! It must be going to storm tonight,' she is also feeling the oppressiveness of Medvyedenko's presence, as well as of her own hopeless feelings for Konstantin, who is in love with Nina—of which fact Medvyedenko has only just reminded her! However, given such close thundery weather, a summer's evening and a setting down on the edge of the lake, the director may consider that it is very probable there will be gnats which will serve as a further irritation to Madame Arkadina, who is already in a bad temper and determined to wreck the evening. But it is during the performance of Konstantin's play that Chekov has provided the perceptive director with a clue to further accidental comedy. It lies in the tiny detail of the sulphur which Konstantin burns as an effect to suggest the devil. It is exactly at this point that the performance of Konstantin's play peters out, and no wonder! If there is one thing calculated to break up any gathering it is the burning of sulphur, which brings tears to the eyes, causing one to retch, cough and choke. More-over, in his enthusiasm, it is quite likely that Konstantin has overdone it and used too much!

In the second act of this play it is midday. The men are out in the fields harvesting. It is high summer. It is essential to capture the feeling of intense heat and the lassitude that it creates. Everyone will be seated in the shade of trees, lying in hammocks, sheltered under parasols. There must be a stillness and the shimmering reflections of the sunlight on the lake. But it is a surface calm, and with the entry of Shamrayev, hot, sweaty and dusty from the cornfields, the tension snaps and the passions that have been submerged erupt and flash like a summer's storm. After this upheaval we have once again the still-ness of heat, the perfume of flowers, the vastness of the lake with all its islands, the cool-ness of trees, the sense of sky overhead—'How beautiful it is!' murmurs Trigorin.

It is in the following scene between Trigorin and Nina that Chekov articulates the magpie mentality of the artist and, at the same time, demonstrates its negative aspects, its excesses:

'Even now while talking to you I can't forget that there is an unfinished story waiting in my room. Do you see that cloud? Looks remarkably like a grand piano, doesn't it? The moment I saw it I thought, I mustn't forget to mention somewhere in my story that a cloud looking like a grand piano sailed across the sky. I catch a whiff of heliotrope: A-ha, I say to myself, quick, make a mental note: a sickly smell, the widow's colour—must mention that in a description of a summer evening. I snap up every word, every sentence you or I utter just for the sake of locking them away in my literary lumber-room—they may come in useful one day! . . . And so it goes on and on, and I find no rest from myself. I feel I am consuming my own life . . .'

It was Robert Frost who said, 'You don't take notes during a love affair'—by which he meant that there must come a time when the artist must cease observing clinically and rather must observe intuitively. He must become submerged momentarily in a personal experience of life.

So it is that with the antennae of his senses the director records the rough material of his craft, whether walking in the country and observing the different quality of light from that in the town or the way sunlight through windows throws changing patterns of luminosity on a wall; listening to people talking in a hotel, or observing the way a voice echoes as it carries down or up the shaft of a dumb waiter; visiting museums, art galleries, antique shops, reading and looking, listening and learning.

A play is like a large country house with many rooms, only a few of which are on view to the public, and yet the audience must be able to sense the other rooms and the gardens beyond. It is in the power of the actor, exercising his imagination and working upon the imaginative response of the audience, to deepen our understanding of ourselves and of one another. As Harley Granville Barker once wrote, 'There is far more to our enjoyment of a play than the mere looking and listening. Its performance, both on our part and the actors', is an exercise in social and human relationships.'

11 Reflections

If an actor has a soliloquy or a long speech and the stage is full of actors and the director cannot invent a reason for the other actors to leave the stage, he may be able to employ the device of freezing the surrounding action, leaving only the central actor free to move. He may further heighten this effect by dimming down the lights and concentrating only on the one actor.

The device of freezing action on stage in order to isolate and focus attention upon a central character has been used with especial effect by Tyrone Guthrie. The one important thing is that the actors, having frozen into a characteristic pose as in a painting, should not blink! The secret is to fix the eyes upon some focal point or thought and not to let the concentration waver. If the actor merely stops moving and thinks to himself, 'I've got to stand still for three minutes and not blink,' then his eyes will smart with tears, his face itch and in some part of his body a muscle will tense and begin to ache.

The actress who plays Hermione in *The Winter's Tale*, in which she has to pose as a statue for some considerable length of time in the last act, will need to rehearse this from the start if she is to acquire total control over her body. She will need to learn how to minimize her breathing, and here the design of the dress can help to conceal any involuntary movements at the chest or throat.

If in a scene the actors in the background are supposed to be carrying on other conversations it is important that these should be actual conversations in character and not the traditional murmur of 'Bread and butter, bread and butter', but the actors must guard against becoming so carried away that they become vocally dominant and intrude upon the main action of the play. In pauses during the action of the play, however, it creates an added authenticity to be suddenly able to overhear fragments of conversation.

In such a scene they should not stand or pose self-consciously as though afraid to distract from the main action. The more naturalistic their behaviour, the more successfully will they fade into the background. Yet they must remember that any sudden movement will at once attract and distract an audience's attention. If an actor has to move suddenly let him do it in a pause or between speeches.

Audiences today are more used to looking than listening; therefore they are easily attracted or distracted by the visual. The imaginative director will learn to capitalize on this.

Realistic business can often take up too much time on the stage, and therefore the director has to foreshorten it, remembering that theatre is not reality itself but the illusion of reality. It is for the director to select his effects and thereby create an impression of reality.

The director has to remember that realistic business only holds an audience when it is either advancing the action or revealing character.

In blocking a play on a proscenium-arch stage it can help to block as though the production were being staged in the round. This will add a three-dimensional depth to the grouping. At a later stage the director can clean up the grouping so that there is no masking.

The actor's eyes are as immediate as cats' eyes at night. If an actor speaks with closed eyes he is likely to alienate an audience. The effect would be similar to that of being in the presence of a blind man. Similarly, if an actor plays with his eyes downcast we shall tend to look down on him, thinking, 'Why doesn't he look us in the eye?' It may be that the actor in question is terrified of the fourth wall and the thought of all the people out front watching him. It is one of the paradoxes of acting that the actor has to behave as in real life yet modify his behaviour so that it may be easily observed by several hundred people seated on various levels in front of him. He has to act to the stalls and to the gallery yet give the impression that he is totally unaware of them.

The eyes of the actor are like binoculars. Through them the audience sees into the inner state of the character. As in real life, a man may be joking and making people think he is in the best of spirits yet his eyes betray his inner loneliness, anguish, indecision or fatigue.

If an actor cannot arrive at the emotion of a scene the director may need to suggest that he think of an equivalent moment in his own life when he lost someone, was first in love, broke down or suffered a shock. The actor may then choose to do an improvisation on this moment. The object of the exercise is to recall the emotion experienced at a similar moment in his own life and then apply this to the scene in question.

When a person suffers shock he does not at once burst into tears. The effect of shock is to numb a person so that he feels nothing. Only later, as the shock wears off, does the emotion flood back and the person break down.

Although everything in this book is based upon good acting practice, every statement is capable of one or more qualifications. Yet to do this would make for dull reading. Every principle, every practice, is subject to the imagination, talent and temperament of the individual actor and the requirements of the moment.

What is offered is a counsel of perfection. One has to have an ideal of which to fall short!

There are some actors who put so much energy into getting into character off-stage that they have nothing left by the time they come on!

To discover the life of a character before the play begins is only of value in so far as it helps the actor towards a more truthful characterization and a greater depth in performance.

Stanislavski never intended his Method to become a Cult.

Even Lee Strasberg has said, 'There is no one Method. There are merely many methods of acting, and my task is to help each actor find his own method.'

When playing a complex or demanding rôle the actor needs to put himself into a state of preparation beforehand. He has to put aside his own worries and concerns and, as in a state of trance, let the character take over.

Too often an actor uses the first act of a play in order to warm up and only gets going by the third act. To arrive early at the theatre and to prepare for performance is essential.

The extrovert actor will spend the time before the show visiting other actors in their dressing-rooms and chatting. He, too, in his own way, is warming up and getting ready for the performance—even if in the process he drives his fellow actors mad!

In between scenes and each time he comes off stage the actor must maintain a continuity of thought and feeling so that there is no break in his performance. However, he does not have to be intense about this!

In a sense the actor who is playing a major rôle is preparing all day for his performance that night. He may be at lunch, playing tennis, reading, but always at the back of his mind is the thought of the performance ahead. The whole day is directed towards this end. The actor is a man who must of necessity lead a double life. He is like a married man waiting to visit his mistress.

A creative actor will reflect critically upon his performance each night. Sir Donald Wolfit felt that, 'For the actor each night is a fresh start, like a painter wiping out one canvas and starting afresh. If he was less good tonight he has the consolation that tomorrow he may be better.'

Martha Graham once said, 'We are the servants of the public and we cannot foresee what will be the effect of our performance upon them. This ought to keep us humble.'

Eleanora Duse received after a performance a torn scrap of paper from an obviously poor woman. On it were written the words, 'Your voice, just your voice, has tonight given me fresh hope!'

The art of comedy is the art of seriousness.

You cannot play farce with your tongue in your cheek.

Farce is larger than life, and yet still recognizably life.

To laugh at one's own jokes on stage is invariably as fatal as to feel sorry for oneself in a tragedy. Both alienate an audience.

If there is a laugh in the middle of a line and another at the end it is better to kill the laugh in the middle for the sake of a bigger laugh at the end.

The art of throwing away a line in order to get a bigger laugh is to speak a preposterous or funny line as casually as though one were saying, 'Well, I'm going up to bed.'

The secret of playing the witticisms of Wilde is to pretend that they are not witty. A note of elegant boredom should be sounded. His lines should be thrown away with the nonchalance of his own gesture of smoking expensive cigarettes and after two puffs throwing them away. The point of this gesture is the expensiveness of the cigarettes. The common failing is to smoke the expensive cigarette to the end and choke everyone with the heady aroma of Turkish tobacco!

In real life people often start to speak before another person has finished speaking. So, too, in the theatre an actor will sometimes tread on cues—especially if there is an underlying sense of excitement, curiosity or tension to a scene. For one actor to speak and the others to answer after a short pause and so on, line–pause, line–pause, indicates gentility. While sometimes this may be the effect aimed at in a scene, it can be deadly dull if carried through a whole production!

The director is like a conductor. He has to study the score. It is his understanding of the sub-text that will suggest the rhythm, tempo and pitch of a scene.

Listen to a rehearsal with your eyes closed or your back turned to the actors and judge how well the actors' voices command your attention and interest.

A change of thought requires a change of voice, of inflection, tone, pitch, rhythm or tempo.

Too often actors cannot distinguish between a full stop, a comma, a colon, a semicolon, a question, an exclamation mark, parenthesis brackets or a main clause and a subsidiary clause.

It is only when an actor has mastered the technique of speaking that he can use the monotone without the risk of being monotonous. Sarah Bernhardt knew how to use the monotone to great effect.

The greater part of acting, as with all art, is a bag of tricks. It is for the artist to use them to such effect that the audience does not perceive the artifice.

When Alec Guinness spoke Hamlet's soliloquy, 'To be or not to be', he moved in a straight line from upstage to downstage and spoke the words so swiftly and simply that one had the impression of listening to Hamlet thinking. It took one wholly by surprise. Only afterwards did it register how skilfully and musically was the blank verse spoken.

People are not for ever talking in real life, mercifully! Often there are pauses, broken sentences, moments for reflection or for performing a task; moments of embarrassment or boredom. So, too, in the drama. Find the pauses.

If an audience becomes restless in a pause it is either that the pause is unreal, not lived in by the actor, or else it is too long in terms of theatre time. A pause is like a balloon—it must be filled.

What is theatre time? Ultimately it is an actor's or a director's instinct as to what will hold an audience, instinct refined by experience. In *An Ideal Husband* Margaret Lockwood and Michael Denison ceased talking for a minute and a half—a long time in the theatre—to listen to a Schubert song. Their acting in this pause held the audience. Two minutes, however, would have been too long.

In *Private Lives* Rosemary Martin and Edward de Souza held a pause of two and a half minutes while they listened to a recording of Charles Trenet singing *La Mer*. What they did in that time held the audience absorbed, amused and intrigued. A minute less in this instance would not have been time enough.

Virginia Woolf wrote, 'I want to write books about silence, about the things people do not say.' The lines of dialogue on a printed page follow on one after the other. In the theatre there may be, as in music, a pause of one or several beats between one phrase and another.

Conversely, to have too many pauses can make a production seem to have an impediment.

In a Pinter play observe how the sound of water being poured into a glass, a door opening, footsteps crossing a hall, plus the movements of a hand lighting a cigarette, tracing a ladder in a stocking, one leg crossing another are all interwoven into the speaking of the dialogue. Sounds and movements added to the dialogue go to make up the complex score of a production.

William Poel, by getting his actors to speak swiftly, emphasizing only the key words, revolutionized the speaking of Shakespeare. If the actor luxuriates and indulges in a long speech the audience is likely to lose the thread of the argument or the cumulative impact of the images.

A poet does not require the lily to be gilded. The speech should be spoken 'trippingly upon the tongue'. The poet has put the emotion into the choice and arrangement of the words, images, sounds and rhythms. To speak the speech simply is often the most effective. To elaborate and dwell on cadences and images can cause the actor to stand between the listener and the poet, obscuring the view.

Few actors know how to speak poetry. They all want to *Act* it.

Given a long poetic speech, some actors will start to throw their hands about while their heads roll, jerk and nod like demented mandarins. As an exercise, let the actor put his hands into his pockets and stand with a book on his head. At once all the energy that would have gone into the gesticulating goes into the delivery of the lines. He speaks with emphasis, rhythm, variety and clarity. Let him repeat the exercise, allowing himself to make three gestures only. He will immediately feel the benefit of this and be excited. Two days later he will be back at his old tricks. The director must persevere. Technique is not acquired easily.

When speaking poetry, especially on television, the actor should learn to keep his head still. Every movement distracts from the listener's concentration upon the words. This also presupposes that the actor should know the poems by heart. The only movements permitted should be those intended by the actor to emphasize a particular word or phrase.

This economy of movement, in which the speaker is more like a singer, is the style that should be aimed at in the great rhetorical dramas. You cannot act *Samson Agonistes* naturalistically.

Technique is the acquisition of certain skills. Sincerity alone is not enough.

No amount of true feeling will compensate an audience for inaudibility.

About two-thirds of the way through rehearsal it can be helpful to the actors to have a word rehearsal. Everyone sits or lies around comfortably and speaks the dialogue quietly. There should be no attempt to project. The object of the exercise is to ponder the play as a whole, and to think about it in detail. Not having to project or move around, the actors listen attentively to the play, letting it wash over them. Such a rehearsal invariably brings new insights, new subtleties.

In his book *Around the Next Corner*, Denys Blakelock describes how Ernest Thesiger, when rehearsing the part of the ghillie in Barrie's play *Mary Rose*, went to great trouble to acquire an authentic Hebridean accent. But it was such a special kind of accent that it was dismissed by the critics as not coming from Scotland at all!

And now here, in essence, are some reflections by a contemporary of Stanislavski, the great Russian director, Meyerhold.

The director must be bold in his approach. Timidity or hesitancy will not inspire confidence in his actors.

Because the director tells an actor he is satisfied with what he has done one day, it does not necessarily mean that he will be satisfied with it the next.

Tragedy does not mean tears. The voice should be dry.

An actor must have a firm basic structure on which to build his rôle, but this must allow for bits of improvisation. His motivation does not change, but he may find variations each night, according to his own feelings and external influences.

An actor's performance should appear effortless to the audience. Do not spoil it by exaggeration in voice or movement.

Stand as close to the door as possible if you want your exit to be effective. A climax can be ruined if your progress to the door is too lengthy, both in time and distance.

At rehearsal the actor must learn to use objects to reflect what he is thinking and feeling and not handle them automatically.

An actor must be as aware of time and timing as a musician is.

It is essential that the director should really feel the dramatic climaxes of a play.

And finally,

Harley Granville Barker once wrote to John Gielgud:

'For a foundation of criticism technical knowledge is needed.'

To stage a production is to live in terror, to delight in anguish; it is what Paul Valéry calls 'the tragedy of execution'. It means administering to the spiritual welfare of the playwright and at the same time taking into account the temporal seeds of the theatre; establishing the point of view of one evening and of eternity; handling the text of a play, hand in hand with the author, as if it were a magic formula. Directing is the opposite of criticism: the critics, zigzagging between laws and rules on one side and their own pleasure on the other, navigate in the theatre by trying to sound their reactions with an old fathom-stick in one hand and with the other sighting the play through a pair of old marine glasses. Staging a play is the exact opposite of this. It means constantly searching for reasons that will explain liking and admiration. It means living according to poets' rules. It means comporting with the gods of the stage, with the mystery of the theatre. It means being honest and straightforward in the art of pleasing. And sometimes, too, it means making mistakes.

LOUIS JOUVET

Index numbers in italics refer to illustrations